# History of Cambodia

*A Captivating Guide to Cambodian History, Including Events Such as the Rise and Decline of the Khmer Empire, Siege of Angkor, Cambodian-Vietnamese War, and Cambodian Civil War*

# Free Bonus from Captivating History
## (Available for a Limited time)

Hi History Lovers!

Now you have a chance to join our exclusive history list so you can get your first history ebook for free as well as discounts and a potential to get more history books for free! Simply visit the link below to join.

Captivatinghistory.com/ebook

Also, make sure to follow us on Facebook, Twitter and Youtube by searching for Captivating History.

# Contents

# Introduction

Cambodia was, and still is, a country in crisis. At its height, it had a thriving economy, but today, it is tenuous. The people were once well fed, despite having to deal with a cycle of torrential rains during the wet season and spells of dry weather. However, today, the country depends upon the generosity of international donors and help from the United Nations. How did this happen?

Cambodia, or Kampuchea as it was sometimes called in history, was a frequent battleground for other countries besides its own. Still, it had much to call its own. Cambodia had carefully irrigated farmlands and drainage systems, along with systems to provide water during the dry periods. As early as the $12^{th}$ century, it had hospitals that treated its people with natural medicines and remedies. They had a vigorous maritime trade, canals, and even floating cities, from where they sold their products all over the country. They had a strong empire to call their own—that of the Khmer Empire. It is remembered as one of the greatest societies on the Indochinese Peninsula.

Unfortunately, the majority of the folklore of the olden days has been all but forgotten, with their legends fading into the dust of history. Even the names of some of the revered kings of Cambodia have sunk into anonymity. It perhaps doesn't help that Cambodia's early history wasn't recorded by the Cambodian people themselves; they were related second-hand by traveling traders from China. Historian Claude Jacques (1700–1750) said, "Very basic historical mistakes have been made" in regards to Cambodian history because its history prior to the 12ᵗʰ century was based on Chinese inscriptions. When new inscriptions were found, researchers preferred to adjust the newly discovered facts to the initial outline rather than call the Chinese reports into question.

But why didn't the Cambodians record their own history in a more coherent fashion? These were people who battled with the seasons, which fluctuated from monsoons to parched dry periods. What's more, they were badly in need of good management and an orderly society. They had that for a while under some of their early kings. To exacerbate matters, though, it seems they were "surrounded by assassins," as other leaders and neighboring countries had their own hidden agenda.

Victimized for years by antagonistic neighbors, the Cambodians begged for help from France. They were then betrayed by their beneficent French protectors, who turned tyrannical. But why and how did that happen?

It is up to the reader to determine whether Cambodia was a country bent on achieving power and privilege for itself or a suicidal civilization bent on its own self-destruction in hopes of attaining a utopia of its own making.

# Chapter 1 – Early History of Cambodia

## Prehistory and Early History

### Laang Spean Archaeological Site

Hoabinhian stone tools were found by archaeologists from the Franco-Cambodian Prehistoric Mission in a cave in northwestern Cambodia. Carbon dating tests estimate they date back to 6000 or 7000 BCE. Hoabinhian refers to a geological period when the glaciers were first receding, which would allow for human habitation. These Hoabinhian artifacts include "flaked" tools, with stones having been chipped or scraped to produce points. Prehistoric pottery was also found there, dating back to 4200 BCE.

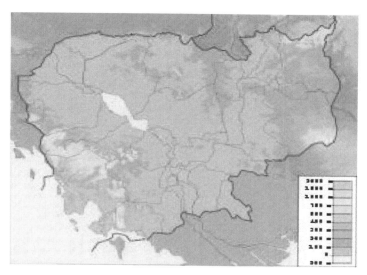

Area of Archaeological Site at Laang Spean (Yellow)

*https://en.wikipedia.org/wiki/Laang_Spean#/media/File:Cambodia_relief_map.svg*

## Samrong Sen Site

Stone Implements and Ceramics at Samrong Sen

*Muséum de Toulouse, CC BY-SA 4.0 <https://creativecommons.org/licenses/by-sa/4.0>, via Wikimedia Commons https://commons.wikimedia.org/wiki/File:Samrong_Sen_Vase_MHNT.PRE.2013.0.579.jpg*

Stone Implements and Ceramics at Samrong Sen

*Muséum de Toulouse, CC BY-SA 4.0 <https://creativecommons.org/licenses/by-sa/4.0>, via Wikimedia Commons https://commons.wikimedia.org/wiki/File:Ciseau_poli_MHNT_PRE_2004_0_132_Moura_S omrong_Sen.jpg*

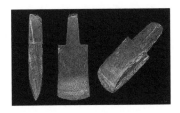

Stone Implements and Ceramics at Samrong Sen

Stone Implements and Ceramics at Samrong Sen

At the base of Tonle Sap, a huge lake in western Cambodia, flows the Stueng Chinit River, where several excavations have been conducted by local villagers and the French protectorate of Cambodia in the mid-19th century. A 20th-century excavation yielded prehistoric implements that date to between 3400 BCE and 500 CE. Two of the excavations yielded artifacts, which included armbands, beads, undecorated pottery, and drinking vessels. Skulls and human bones were also discovered, which have been dated to 1500 BCE.

Phum Snay Site

The archaeological site of Phum Snay was discovered in northwestern Cambodia and was excavated by the Australian National University. It is believed the site was first active in the year 500 BCE and fell into disuse around 500 CE. The researchers from the university discovered human remains in a number of burial sites, along with bronze artifacts and semi-precious stones.

Skeletal remains show signs of cranial injuries caused by blunt force trauma, suggesting that this site may have housed a number of warring villages. Some bodies were simply stretched out and placed in pits, while others were buried with ceramic vessels and decorative items, such as rings and bells. Animal bones were also found buried in the dirt, and it was suggested by historians that this may imply sacrificial slaughters of animals accompanied the burial rites. In the graves, iron and bronze tools were found in addition to weapons, which included daggers, swords, spearheads, and other projectile points.

There was also evidence of dental caries (tooth decay) in the human remains. This gives researchers a glimpse into the dietary habits of these early people. It's interesting to note that there was a difference between the males and the females, as the female remains often had more cavities. Researchers have theorized that the males tended to eat more protein-based food, while the females ate more "cariogenic" foods, that is, more starch and carbohydrates. It has been suggested that the reason behind this was the fact women spent more time working in the fields near the vegetable crops while the men were out hunting.

DNA studies of the human remains found at Phum Snay resemble that of modern-day humans from not only Cambodia but also Thailand, Vietnam, and Laos. According to the journal *Anthropological Science*, examinations of the skeletal remains uncovered at Phum Snay reveal the dental features of the skulls were akin to those of Austronesian ancestors, but some show other evidence of origins from populations farther north, even as far north as Tibet.

## Oc Eo Site

This site, now located in Vietnam, was once part of Cambodia. At that site, archaeologists unearthed tools, jewelry, casts for making jewelry, coins, and religious statuary. The coins appear to be imitations of the kind used by Rome during the 1st century, so it has been conjectured that the ancient Romans traversed the area on their way to China, where they sought to open up diplomatic relations.

Scholars indicate that Oc Eo was also a cultural and economic area essential for early Funan development (Funan was an early kingdom that covered parts of Cambodia, Thailand, and Vietnam). There, it was said, traders and craftsmen met and exchanged goods and taught the locals various skills.

## Ethnic and Language Groups in Ancient Cambodia

One of the factors used in determining the identity of ancient or indigenous cultures of a region is language. Sanskrit was the classical language of the countries in Southeast Asia. It originated in the Indian subcontinent, the heart of Hinduism and Buddhism. Sanskrit was mostly a spoken language at that time, but it became a written language in the 1st millennium BCE, at least according to surviving evidence. Other language families of Southeast Asia in ancient times were Indo-Iranian and Indo-Aryan. Indo-Aryan is a subgroup of the Indo-European language family, specifically identified with India, although it spread throughout all of South Asia. Pali, an Indo-Aryan language, was also spoken in Cambodia, but it was used primarily for religious purposes.

The foremost Western expert on Cambodian history, David Chandler, said, "Sanskrit inscriptions, in verse, praise the actions of kings and the elite, such as building Hindu temples." Sanskrit was the language and text of the upper classes. It marked the difference between "those who grew rice" and those who did not. When a person mastered Sanskrit, it was said they were "rescued from the mud," meaning they weren't among those who worked in the rice paddies. It was possible to climb the ladder and reach a more elite status, but that didn't happen often.

## The Funan Kingdom

The first known polity of Cambodia was the Funan Kingdom. Historians estimate that Funan existed from the $1^{st}$ century CE to the $6^{th}$ century CE. The term "Funan" means "Mountain Kingdom" in Khmer. The name was given to this state, which covered the southern tip of the Indochinese Peninsula, by two itinerant Chinese cartographers, who were also traders and diplomats. Funan was described as an "Indianized" state, meaning it was influenced by Indian culture. However, it was more a collection of loose communities rather than a proper state. Those communities were united by religion and the economy, and they depended upon rice as their prime commodity. It isn't known what the people who lived there called themselves or their region, which is why historians use the term "Funan" to refer to them.

Linguists have stated that the language of the people who settled in Funan spoke, for the most part, Mon-Khmer. This is an Austroasiatic language, and it is also the indigenous language of Thailand (called the Kingdom of Siam in the early days) and Myanmar. Since the majority of the people spoke Mon Khmer, scholars believe most of the people were Khmers, although they claim it is possible that Austronesian-speaking peoples might have been present as well. In prehistorical days, the Austronesian people were a seafaring group who populated maritime Southeast Asia, including modern-day Taiwan and Oceania. The Austronesians invented very early sailing vessels like catamarans.

## Mythological Foundations

The earliest people of the land believed the sun and moon were deities, much like other cultures around the world. Funan has an ancient legend regarding a foreigner by the name of Huntian. As the story relates, Huntian arrived in the land of Funan and desired a dragon princess. The term "dragon princess" comes from the teachings in one of the Vedic Sanskrit narrations, the *Rig Veda*. As the legend states, Huntian shot a magic arrow into the princess's boat, which reportedly frightened her into marrying him. In exchange, the girl's father "enlarged the possessions of his son-in-law by drinking up the water that covered the country, thus exposing the land." This myth was passed to Cambodia from India.

Some scholars believe Huntian is the same figure as Kaundinya, whose tales are marked in Sanskrit inscriptions. However, there are disputes among scholars about that assignation, as there is a difference in syllables. Huntian is also known by the name Preah Thong in the Khmer culture, the vernacular language of the Cambodians.

According to the Chinese *Book of Liang*, "The people of the Funan kingdom originally had the custom of going naked, tattooing their bodies and letting their hair hang down." As the narration continued, it said that the Funan ruler was a female named Liuye. She is perhaps better known as Queen Soma, the daughter of the king of the Nagas, but she was also known as Neang Neak in Khmer. The "Nagas" are serpent beings in Buddhist mythology. A Hindu brahman, or priest of the gods, named Huntian (Kaundinya) surprised her with his unannounced arrival. As the story goes on, "Huntian taught Liuye to make a hole in a piece of cloth and put her head through it, using it as clothing to cover her body." Another version relates that Huntian shot an arrow at Liuye's ship when she tried to pillage his vessel. Either way, she gave herself up to him, and they became husband and wife, the first royal couple of Funan.

In the 1st century, Queen Soma and King Kaundinya reigned over Funan. Eventually, the land was segmented into many kingdoms, one of which became today's Cambodia.

### The Culture and Lifestyle of Funan

The Funan Kingdom arose in the Mekong Delta on the southern tip of the Indochinese Peninsula, encompassing all of current-day

Cambodia, segments of Thailand to the north, and Vietnam to the east. Therefore, Funan covered the strategically important coastline along the South China Sea to the east and the Bay of Thailand and the Bay of Bengal to the west.

A temple in Funan

*Tonbi ko, CC BY-SA 4.0 <https://creativecommons.org/licenses/by-sa/4.0>, via Wikimedia Commons https://commons.wikimedia.org/wiki/File:Wat_asram_moha_russei.jpg*

Two theories have been promulgated about the location of Funan's capital. It may have been near today's town of Banam or possibly a town known as Vyadhapura ("City of the Hunter"). Funan was divided into city-states made up of residential villages. The people raised rice and root crops, and irrigation and the draining of wet terraces were made more systemic as time went on.

The king's dwelling had "double terraces," with palisades around it instead of walls. The roof was made of algae. Elephants were the kings' primary means of transport. As the people further developed villages, they began to war with each other. Slaves were often taken after these raids.

The lords of these villages felt they needed the divine protection of Shiva, the deity of rebirth. Thus, the people believed in reincarnation. They had ascetic brahmans who wandered the villages, teaching the people about devotion to Shiva and imparted the notions of karma. Karma is based on a person's behavior; a person who performs good acts has a good future, while those who don't suffer the consequences of their negative actions. The goal of Hinduism is a release from one's physical and mental suffering and an end to the repeated cycles of rebirth in the human state.

Sanskrit was the royal language of Funan, while Mon-Khmer was the language the majority of the people spoke. Taxes were paid in gold, silver, perfumed wood, or pearls. The brahmans were educated and had large book collections. Both Hinduism and, to some extent, Buddhism thrived in Funan. The ancient *Book of Liang*, complied by Yao Sillian, indicates that King Rudravarman (6th century CE) requested copies of the texts from the Chinese when traders visited, which serves as proof of Funan's interest in Buddhism.

Funan depended upon trade via the Maritime Silk Road and reached its height during the 3rd century CE under King Fan Shiman. Under him, Funan had a large fleet and a complex bureaucracy based on a tribute system. If a polity, such as Funan, wished to conduct trade with other nations, it would send envoys to those emperors or kings, kowtow to them, and acknowledge their superiority and precedence, who would then grant permission to conduct trade. The Indian Ocean trade routes, sometimes called the "Monsoon Marketplace," connected Funan to India via the Gulf of Siam (current-day Gulf of Thailand), through the Andaman Sea and the Bay of Bengal. In the east, the vessels would move along the Isthmus of Kra in Malay, take a coastland journey along the Gulf of Thailand, and then travel around the Mekong Delta, hugging the coast of Vietnam to reach China. That route, called the Trans-Asiatic route, was an off-shoot of the larger Maritime Silk Road. Exports from Funan were forest products, gold, elephants, rhinoceros' horns, ivory, kingfisher feathers, and spices.

Oc Eo was a Funan port of call. It had a series of vertical and horizontal canals that led to Ta Keo in Cambodia, so it was most likely used as a trade route. Due to the buildup of sediment over the many years, Oc Eo is no longer a port. According to the ancient geographers, it bore the name "Kattigara."

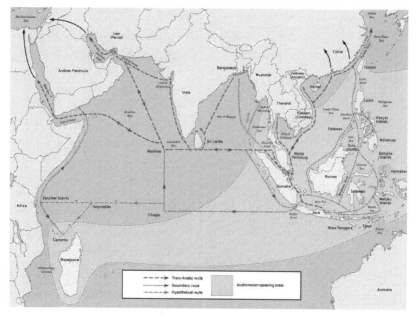

The Maritime Silk Road

In the lowlands of Funan, the wet monsoon season, which lasted between May and October, brought driving rains to the southwest. The Chinese annals called Funan a "realm wrested from the mud." The people lived in stilt houses and cultivated rice paddies. From December to April, it was (and still is) the dry monsoon season, which brought sunny and hot weather, especially in January and February.

It was said that Hun Pan-huang was the son of Kaundinya I (Preah Thong or Huntian) and Queen Soma. The fifth ruler (if one includes Queen Soma), Fan Shiman, "had large ships built, and sailing all over the immense sea, he attacked more than ten kingdoms. He extended his territory five or six thousand li [about 1,553 square miles]." Funan reached its peak during Fan Shiman's reign in the early 3rd century CE. He created a feudal society and sent ambassadors to China and

India in the interests of trade and diplomacy. The Indianization of Funan most likely occurred during this time.

It is believed that Fan Shiman established a small trade monopoly in the region. The people were rather well-to-do at the time, as they used silver utensils. Taxes were paid in pearls, perfumes, and gold.

The Funan Kingdom ended after Rudravarman's death circa 545 CE. However, some historians dispute this, basing the end of the kingdom on a single remark made in the Chinese annals from the Sui dynasty. According to these historians, Rudravarman was succeeded by Bhavavarman I, whose reign ran until circa 590 CE. It further states that his successor was his brother, Chitrasena, who styled himself as King Mahendravarman. Yet another theory states that Chitrasena and Bhavavarman I together conquered the Funan Kingdom and created the Chenla Kingdom. The ancient inscriptions say that Bhavavarman I conquered Funan "at the tip of a sword."

There are several theories about why Funan collapsed. Some say the Trans-Asiatic sea route was supplanted by trade with the island of Sumatra, which was farther south of Funan. If that was the case, Funan would have needed to establish overland trade in order to dominate the region. Given the competition of these kingdoms, that wouldn't have been an easy undertaking.

## Chenla Kingdom – 6ᵗʰ Century to 802 CE

Most historians believe that Bhavavarman I was not a part of the ruling dynasty of Funan. They think he expanded Cambodia after he conquered Funan. However, as mentioned above, this is disputed among scholars. And the disagreements don't end there, as there are claims that Chenla, also known as Zhenla, never existed as a centralized kingdom. Modern historians indicate that Chenla was actually a loose confederation of principalities.

Bhavavarman I followed the tradition of Shaivism, a branch of Hinduism that recognizes the deity, Shiva, as the supreme being. Shiva is seen as the creator and destroyer of life. Shaivism embraces an ascetic form of life and values the practice of yoga as a means to be one with Shiva. Shiva is sometimes represented along with Vishnu, who is considered the preserver of life. In the year 590 CE, Bhavavarman I was succeeded by Chitrasena, who took the name Mahendravarman I. In view of the fact that there were sometimes hostilities among Indochinese countries, Mahendravarman sent an ambassador to the neighboring kingdom of Champa to ensure cordial relations.

The height of the Chenla Kingdom occurred under King Isanavarman, who followed Mahendravarman. Isanavarman ruled over the Chenla Kingdom from 616 to 637 CE. An inscription during his reign states, "The great King Isanavarman is full of glory and bravery. He is the King of Kings, who rules over Suvarnabhumi until the sea, which is the border, while the kings in the neighboring states honor his order to their heads." Isanavarman conquered some principalities in northwestern Cambodia and made his capital Isanapura. A Hindu temple complex called Sambor Prei Kuk is believed to have been Isanapura, and today, it is a UNESCO World Heritage Site, located in Kampong Thom Province. Much of the complex was destroyed during the subsequent wars that ravaged Cambodia, but there were originally 150 temples and sacred buildings at the site.

People were expected to make donations at these sacred places. Those included goods, land, and slaves, which would be given to the king. Taxes were collected at the temples, including minor ones. Since lands were donated, their grounds became larger. It did, however, subtract valuable farmland from the commoners. The temples served to attract more business from foreigners and add to the prestige of the kingdom. The construction of the temples required sandstone, which looks quite elegant but is heavy. Therefore, a lot of slaves were needed to haul it.

Religion

Buddhism, which also originated in India, was practiced in Cambodia as well. Although the people of Cambodia originally observed Hindu, historians conjecture that Buddhism traveled to Cambodia via the traders on the Maritime Silk Road. The two religions coexisted peaceably in the country. Twentieth-century Indian historian Himanshu Prabha Ray indicated that Buddhism was more common among those who partook in the Maritime Silk Road, while Brahmic Hinduism was prevalent among farmers. Deities, such as Brahma, Krishna, Indra, and Lakshmi, were worshiped, and their statuary exists among the ruins of sacred sites.

Shiva

**Buddha**

*https://commons.wikimedia.org/wiki/File:Gandhara_Buddha_(tnm).jpeg*

According to historians, the kings did not enforce Hinduism, Buddhism, or any other religion upon their people.

The Hindus used cremation to dispose of deceased persons. The crematoriums were devoted to the veneration of members of the brahman caste. Even today, people gather at the burial sites of their ancestors during Pitru Paksha, which lasts for two weeks, where they offer prayers to their deceased loved ones, often bringing them sticky rice balls to feed upon. They pray and call upon their ancestors to accept their gifts of food. If their sins are not too big, the ancestors are allowed to eat the food, which they do only after sunset.

Social Status

As elucidated earlier, the most common languages spoken in Cambodia during the 7th century were Sanskrit and Khmer. Sanskrit was the language of religion, and those who became more learned in Sanskrit were sometimes granted higher positions.

Society wasn't divided along gender lines, but it was separated into the rich and the poor. Women often played important roles in religious rituals. Slavery existed, and the children of slaves would become slaves themselves. If one owed a debt and couldn't pay it off, they worked off the debt through slavery, similar to indentured servants.

## Economy

The economy was based upon wet-rice agriculture and the mobilization of manpower. An extensive irrigation system was built to provide the proper amount of water to the rice paddies and to control run-off. The kingdom produced surpluses of rice, which they traded. In fact, at the ruins of the former seaport Oc Eo, materials from other countries have been found by archaeologists.

## Water and Land Chenla

Jayavarman I ruled Chenla from approximately 657 to 681 CE. Jayavarman left no male heirs, and his daughter, Jayadevi, became the new monarch. Her succession was contested, and many conflicts arose. During her reign, Chenla was split into two: "Water Chenla" and "Land Chenla." Jayadevi deeply lamented these divisions, but she was not able to reunite the kingdom.

Land Chenla referred to the upper region of Cambodia, while Water Chenla was located near the Mekong Delta in the lower area of Cambodia. The two groups split their land based upon the geological features of their territories. The people of Land Chenla reportedly lived a peaceable life, but the people of Water Chenla were subject to attacks from Javanese pirates, who sailed up from their islands that were located south of the Indochinese Peninsula. Java was ruled by the Shailendra dynasty at the time. Shailendra means "King of the Mountain," although the term may have been copied from the Funan people. In the late 8th century, Water Chenla became the vassal of the Shailendra. The last of the Water Chenla kings is believed to have been killed, with his people being incorporated into a polity under the Javanese monarchy, in 790 CE.

There is very little known about Land Chenla, except for the mentions of it during the reign of Jayavarman II. In 802, Jayavarman solidified his kingdom, and he is seen as the founder of the Khmer Empire.

# Chapter 2 – Khmer Empire, 802–1150

The Khmer Empire, also known as the Angkor Empire, existed between 802 and 1431. The word "Angkor" is derived from the Sanskrit word *nagara*, meaning city. Most of the knowledge of the Khmer Empire doesn't come from the written records of its own historians. Instead, it is pieced together from stone inscriptions or steles about the kings, archaeological evidence, narrations by Chinese traders and various diplomats, and bas-reliefs depicting market scenes, palace life, military endeavors, and daily life. For example, knowledge about one of Cambodia's capitals, Indrapura, has come from the Sdok Kok Thom inscription in Thailand.

### Khmer Language

The Khmers of Cambodia spoke a dialect of the Khmer language. Today, Khmer is the official language of Cambodia, with the vast majority speaking Central Khmer. The Khmer people in sections of Thailand speak Surin Khmer (Northern Khmer), and the Khmer people who live in modern-day Vietnam speak Southern Khmer. The three varieties of the language—Central, Northern, and Southern—are mutually intelligible. David Chandler, the eminent Cambodian historian, said, "Khmer inscriptions are all in prose. They record the founding of temples and the details of temple administration." Khmer was the language used for everyday purposes, and it was also one of the most commonly spoken vernacular languages in all of Southeast Asia.

Ancient Khmer Script

*https://commons.wikimedia.org/wiki/File:AncientKhmerScript.jpg*

### The Mon Language

The Mon language is an Austroasiatic language spoken in Myanmar (formerly Burma) and Thailand. It is closely related to the Khmer language. Mon is called a "lingua franca," or "bridge language," as it is a dialect that makes it possible for people with different native languages to communicate with each other.

### Early Kings of the Khmer Empire

In 802 CE, the great ruler Jayavarman II took over what historians call the Khmer Empire (Jayavarman would have called it Kambuja). At the beginning of his reign, he went to a sacred mountain, Mount **Mahendraparvata**, now known as Phnom Kulen, to declare the kingdom's independence. According to David Chandler, Jayavarman II made himself the "universal monarch" and had the ceremony conducted in such a way that "made it impossible for Java to control holy Cambodia." It is not known for certain whether "Java" refers to the island or Champa, a collection of polities in Vietnam. It is even possible it might be referring to something else entirely. According to some scholars, Jayavarman II originally came from the Shailendra court in Java and brought back the culture from that region. Historians have also conjectured that Jayavarman II began his career in Vyadhapura in eastern Cambodia. Archaeological evidence there indicates that he had some relations with the Chams, who lived in the neighboring province of Champa. Since they were a closer threat than the Shailendra, it is quite plausible that the inscription might refer to Champa.

Jayavarman II widened his territory as his reign progressed, allowing for the king to move his capital to Hariharalaya near Cambodia's modern-day town of Rolous. He conquered various territories, including the city of Vyadhapura, Sambhupura, Banteay Prei Nokor, and possibly Wat Pu, which is in present-day Laos.

Jayavarman II's name shows up in several inscriptions (none of which he made himself), but perhaps the most important is the one at the Sdok Kok Thom temple in Thailand. This inscription was made during the 11th century, which was two centuries after Jayavarman died. The writing speaks of the exploits of the Angkor's founding families and their service to the Khmer court and to the chaplains of the Shaivite Hindu religion.

Jayavarman II died in 835, and his successors continued to expand the kingdom. Sadly, there is not much information on the kings of Cambodia who ruled during the 9th century. Epigraphists have said that the only evidence of the three kings who followed Jayavarman II are the names inscribed on steles found at Preah Ko in Hariharalaya. Researchers, such as the noted Cambodian historian Michael Vickery, reported that the contemporaneous inscriptions are the most trustworthy, but there are doubts about the reliability of inscriptions made after that date, including the names and reigns of successive kings and queens.

It has been written that Jayavarman III, who followed his father, Jayavarman II, hunted elephants, but little else was said about him. Jayavarman III died in 877, with Indravarman I taking the throne. He was notable for his building projects, setting the foundation for future rulers. He built the temple of Preah Ko, which he dedicated to his maternal father and grandfather, as well as Jayavarman II, his uncle. Indravarman had a peaceful rule, which was why he was most likely able to commission so many new buildings.

Indravarman died in 889, and his son, Yasovarman I, took over, ruling from 889 to 900. It was said he had leprosy and that he died of the disease; however, it is hard to discern legend from fact when it comes to centuries-old inscriptions.

Yasovarman, the Leper King

*Allie Caulfield, CC BY 2.0 <https://creativecommons.org/licenses/by/2.0>, via Wikimedia Commons https://commons.wikimedia.org/wiki/File:Phnom_Bakheng_relief_(2009).jpg*

Yasovarman founded many monasteries, or *ashrams*. These would serve as rest stops for the king on his journeys. He most notably moved the capital to Yasodharapura (Angkor). There are many reasons why he made this move, although it is believed the major reason was the old capital had become too crowded. Here, there was ample space for new religious monuments. Some of the most famous Cambodian structures, such as Angkor Wat, would be built at Yasodharapura, as it would serve as the capital of the Khmer Empire for the next 600 years. Yasovarman also continued with his predecessor's huge water projects. By this time, the country had a centralized state with royal heads appointed to run the various provinces.

There is not much known about the kings who immediately followed Yasovarman I. King Rajendravarman II, who started his reign in 944, was the next notable king. According to inscriptions from during his reign, Rajendravarman was victorious over Ramanya and Champa. Historians indicate that Ramanya might have been a part of modern-day Thailand. The inscriptions stated that Rajendravarman II's sword was often stained with blood, indicating that he was an experienced and fierce warrior.

### King Jayavarman V and Women Power

Rajendravarman II passed away in 968, and he was succeeded by his ten-year-old son, Jayavarman V. Since he was so young, he didn't truly rule in the early years of his reign, leaving that to the court officials. Jayavarman was a Shaivite, but he tolerated Buddhism, which had begun to flourish in Southeast Asia by the 9th century. Buddhism teaches tolerance for all, and as a result of these beliefs, Jayavarman awarded many women positions in his administration. The Chinese annals indicated that women in Kambuja were noted for their knowledge of astronomy and politics. After Jayavarman V died in 1001, a turbulent period followed. Three kings reigned simultaneously, constantly warring against each other for the throne.

### Suryavarman I

By 1006, Suryavarman I had risen to the throne. It was said that he was not Cambodian by blood but was linked to the Cambodian elite.

Historians theorize that he rose to the throne through local warfare and the formation of coalitions. Suryavarman also established diplomatic relations with the Chola dynasty in southern India. That was fortunate, as he enlisted their aid to help him deal with attacks from the Tambralinga kingdom, located on the Malay Peninsula, and its later ally, the Srivijaya Empire. Religious overtones were involved in these wars because Khmer and Chola were Hindu Shaivites, while Tambralinga and the Srivijaya Empire were Mahayana Buddhists. The Khmer and Chola proved victorious in these conflicts.

Suryavarman fought in many skirmishes with his neighbors, but he was shrewd. When he didn't want to war with a kingdom for control, he formed coalitions by virtue of marriages. Suryavarman moved steadily westward, conquering smaller principalities. He won his final battle "from a king surrounded by other kings," according to the inscriptions found on temple steles. One of his early actions was to require his officials to take oaths of loyalty called *tamvrac*. They would swear, "If all of us...do not keep this oath with regard to His Majesty, may he still reign long, we ask that he inflict on us royal punishment of all sorts."

### Suryavarman II

Under the weight of its internal conflicts and skirmishes with neighboring kingdoms, the Khmer Empire underwent a weak period of central power. An ambitious prince by the name of Suryavarman claimed rights to the throne. One of the inscriptions stated, "He approved the desire of the royal dignity of his family"; in other words, this inscription claims he had a right to assume the throne. However, Suryavarman had to deal with two opposing claimants, Nripatindravarman and Dharanindravarman I, the latter of whom was his great-uncle. Suryavarman, who was "bounding on the head of the elephant of the enemy king...killed him, as Garuda [mystical bird of prey]...would kill a serpent." It is hard to know to which of the two men this inscription refers, but regardless, Suryavarman II took the throne in 1113.

During the reign of King Suryavarman II, the empire attained its greatest geographic extent, as Suryavarman sought to unify the land under his rule.

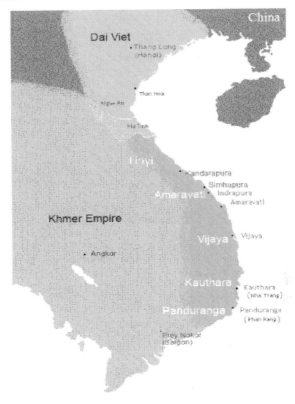

Khmer Empire - Dai Viet and Champa (Champa is green)

*Created by CGlassey, based on maps found in DK Atlas of World History and the Times Atlas of World History., CC BY-SA 3.0 <http://creativecommons.org/licenses/by-sa/3.0/>, via Wikimedia Commons https://commons.wikimedia.org/wiki/File:VietnamChampa1.gif*

## The Dai Viet-Khmer Wars

In 1128, King Suryavarman II demanded tribute payments from Dai Viet, whose current monarch was only about thirteen years old. Dai Viet refused, so Suryavarman decided to exact tribute from them by taking some of their lands, forming an army of 20,000 soldiers in order to do so. He lost the early battles, but he returned with 700 ships the next year. By 1132, Khmer had allied with Champa, which also saw a way to gain new lands. That year, the Khmer Empire and Champa invaded Dai Viet. In 1136, Dai Viet penetrated into Khmer territory and attacked with 30,000 troops. However, they were forced to retreat. War historians have labeled the outcome of this war as inconclusive, as neither side really gained or lost any lands. In addition, after the two monarchs of the respective kingdoms passed, they were both succeeded by weaker rulers.

## The Khmer-Cham Wars

Khmer and Champa had been engaged in conflicts throughout the years, starting back in 950. King Suryavarman II reignited the war in 1145 after the conclusion of the Dai Viet war. After his failure in Dai Viet, Suryavarman II invaded Champa and occupied its capital city, Vijaya. He then destroyed temples at My Son, which was a religious center and the burial site for Champa's royalty.

In the process, Suryavarman II deposed the Cham king, Jaya Indravarman III. The following year, he annexed Champa and put a new king on the throne, who historians believe might have been Suryavarman's brother-in-law. That was short-lived, as the Cham retook the capital and killed the new king. In 1150, Suryavarman tried to take Champa again but was unsuccessful.

## Angkor Wat

Suryavarman II initiated the construction of the magnificent temple complex of Angkor Wat. By land area, it is the largest religious monument in the world.

This temple was originally dedicated to the god Vishnu, the preserver of life. Vishnu's role is to return to Earth during times of great need to restore order and peace within the balance of good and evil. The *Rig Veda*, the sacred Hindu text, says, "Through all this world strode Vishnu: thrice his foot he planted, and the whole world was gathered in his footsteps, Vishnu, the Guardian, whom none deceiveth, made three steps and established his laws."

Rice and other produce were stored in the temples throughout the empire for times of need. Maize, rice, and wheat were collected for the benefit of the state, that is, for the people, as well as for the priests and advisors to the kings. The temples were essentially the basis of the economy, as they acted as distribution centers, receiving goods from the villages and then sending them outward into the local villages. Goods were distributed first to those with power and prestige before being given to those in the countryside.

## The Story of the Churning of the Ocean of Milk

The *devas* (gods) and the *asuras* (demons) stirred up the cosmic ocean—the Kshirasagara—to obtain the *amrita*, or the elixir of immortality. As they churned the ocean, from the great depths arose a deadly poison called Halahala. The poison obscured their sight and filled the sky with choking smoke. The *devas* and *asuras* appealed to the great Shiva for help. Rushing to help his beloved beings on Earth, he swallowed some of the poison to keep it from spreading. The greedy *devas* and *asuras* rushed to snatch the *amrita* when it appeared, clawing and biting each other for it, but Vishnu, disguised as an enchantress named Mohini, coerced the *asuras* to give the potion to "her." Vishnu gave the *amrita* to the *devas*. Svarbhanu, an *asura*, disguised himself as a *deva* and tried to drink of the *amrita*, the holy nectar. Vishnu decapitated him for this deception.

A bas-relief at Angkor Wat depicts this story, and other stories from Hinduism can be found there as well. This particular relief shows the great ocean being churned by the two *asuras* and *devas*. There is also a depiction of the serpent named Vasuki, who Vishnu used to stir up the great waters.

Angkor Wat, Temple Complex of the Khmer Empire

## The Beginning of the Decline

Suryavarman passed away in 1150, perhaps during his campaign against Champa. He was succeeded by Dharanindravarman II, who kicked off a long period of weak rulers.

There were a lot of factors that went into Khmer's demise. For instance, geologists have noted that the water in the area of Angkor Wat was reduced over time and probably became tapped out. The basis of Angkor's rice-based economy depended upon an intricate system of canals and reservoirs. The water provided subsistence for a large population, as there were perhaps as many as 600,000 at Angkor Wat and the surrounding areas alone. The Angkor Wat area reached its height of efficiency during the mid-12th century and started to shrink during the following century.

Lack of maintenance factored into the decline of the empire as well, which was due to the labor shortage during times of war. Weak rulers, civil wars, and the shift from Hinduism to Buddhism also played a role.

# Chapter 3 – The Khmer Empire and the Later Khmer Kingdom, 1150–1600

Not much was written about the immediate successors of Suryavarman. Dharanindravarman II, who was possibly Suryavarman's cousin, took the throne in 1150, and he was followed by Yasovarman II in 1160. According to an inscription, Yasovarman II put down a revolt in the northwest by people who were neither foreigners nor members of the elite; they were depicted as people with "animal heads" in bas-reliefs at the temple of Banteay Chhmar. In 1167, Yasovarman II was assassinated by one of his subordinates, who then seized the throne. That man was Tribhuvanaditya, and he held the throne until 1177.

## Sack of Angkor

The rebellions in the Khmer Empire provided Champa with an opportunity to invade them. In 1170, the Chams attacked, but the outcome of the war was inconclusive. The king of Champa, Jaya Indravarman IV, and his troops tried again in 1177, this time taking the current capital, Yasodharapura (Angkor), and slaughtering Tribhuvanaditya.

A courageous Khmer by the name of Jayavarman rose to defend his country and led a formidable army against the Chams in 1178. After he ousted the Cham invaders, he returned to the capital and found it in chaos and disorder. Jayavarman discovered that the Khmers were embroiled in their own disputes with each, and he put an end to them by 1181. Once that was accomplished, he crowned himself king.

### King Jayavarman VII

Jayavarman VII is considered to be one of Cambodia's greatest kings. He wasn't a legitimate successor to the throne, but he played the part well, as he was very grandiose. Jayavarman VII was a Mahayana Buddhist, which espouses the belief that each person is responsible for his or her own behavior. He was under the impression that he should save his people from suffering. In addition, he tried to integrate Buddhism with the Cambodian ideals of kingship, similar to that of the Hindu monarchs who preceded him.

Since Angkor had been destroyed by the Chams, Jayavarman established a new capital, which he called Angkor Thom. There, he built a magnificent Buddhist temple called the Bayon. There are 216 gigantic faces on the temple, one of whom scholars theorize is of Jayavarman himself. They believe the other faces are of the bodhisattva, who are devout students of Buddha. During its height, Angkor Thom was said to have housed a population of 80,000 to 150,000 people.

The wars between Champa and Cambodia continued for twenty-two more years. In 1203, Jayavarman VII conquered Champa and sacked it. Champa then became a vassal state of the Khmer Empire.

### Beware! They May Bite!

Currently, Angkor Thom has been inflicted with macaque monkeys, which have made the temple their home. Part of the reason for this nuisance was the gradual domestication of the monkeys. To this day, tourists adore seeing them, even though the monkeys will snatch food right out of their hands or even attack people. According to *The Phnom Penh Post,* "These monkeys are no longer afraid of people because people have been feeding them. Now when they don't feed them, the monkeys get upset and steal the food anyway and even bite people." In late 2020, the Cambodian government removed some of the monkeys from the temple complex, but it is almost a certainty that there are still some hanging around.

The Bayon, Angkor Thom

## Ancient Cambodian Medicine

Jayavarman VII not only established a network of roads, including way bridges and rest houses for travelers, but he also endorsed the construction of hospitals. It is written that he "suffered from the illnesses of his subjects more than from his own; the pain that affected men's bodies was for him a spiritual pain, and thus more piercing." Therefore, as part of his grand building projects, he included plans for many hospitals, with Ta Prohm Kel perhaps being the most well-known. The inscription at Ta Prohm Kel records the king's oath: "All the beings who are plunged in the ocean of existence, may I draw them out by virtue of this good work." To future generations, the king added, "May the kings of Cambodia who come after me, attached to goodness...attain with their wives, dignitaries, and friends the place of deliverance where there is no more illness."

Traditional Khmer medicine was a combination of traditional Indian medicine called Ayurveda and ancient Chinese medicine. Archaeologists have noted that these hospitals had a division of labor and included hospital managers, drug grinders, drug distributors, and staff to boil water.

Their medicinal practices were recorded on palm-leaf manuscripts, and although some were inevitably destroyed in conflicts, some have survived to this day. Traditional medicines consisted of plant roots, bark, and leaves, with these medicinal properties being mixed in water. Before administering medication, the staff would pour the mixture over a "Shiva Linga." It represented the assistance of Shiva, who would bring health to the patient.

The *kru pet* were the most educated. The *kru thnam* were herbalists, and the *thmup* were sorcerers. These classes are still around today, but there are only a handful of those belonging to the *kru pet* class. There were a variety of other roles, including bonesetters, diviners, and those who created good luck or love charms. Buddhist monks also played a role, especially if an exorcism was needed.

Ta Prohm Kel - An Early Cambodian Hospital

## Society

The Khmer Empire had a similar caste system as the Hindus. The commoners were toward the bottom, while the kshatriya—the nobles and warriors—were at the top. There were other classes, such as the brahmans (priests) and merchants. The slaves, as one might predict, were at the very bottom. The slaves were usually prisoners captured from wars.

Khmer kings were influenced by the cult of Devaraja, a popular concept in Southeast Asia that promoted the idea that kings were divinely chosen to rule. There were many who supported the king, such as his ministers, servants, and guards. However, most of society was a part of the farming community.

<u>Slaves</u>

The slaves were separated into fourteen categories according to their ethnic origin and duties. Some slaves served as musicians and dancers. Those slaves that serviced temples had a higher status, and they enjoyed a semi-clerical status. All of these people could be bought or sold and given away, as they had no freedom. It appears that many slaves were attached to a place, like a farm, for example, as opposed to being attached to a particular lord.

In addition, there were people who entered servitude to work off a debt. Sometimes parents, due to unfortunate economic hardships, were forced to make their children enter bondage slavery.

Farmers

Farmers dwelled in villages near the rice paddies. Their homes had walls made of bamboo, with thatched roofs. Their houses were on stilts to protect them and their belongings from floods during the monsoon season. According to the book by the Chinese historian and diplomat Zhou Daguan, written in the late 13th century, "the dwellings of the princes and principal officials have a completely different layout and dimensions from those of the people...The official rank of each person determines the size of the houses." Nobles had homes with walls made of bamboo, but their roofs were composed of wooden shingles. Of course, they were also much more elaborate than a common farmer.

Farmers were somewhat free in terms of their livelihood. While they were free to grow rice or vegetables, they weren't free to move elsewhere, as rice paddies were designated for particular farmers.

Farmers and free peasants would be called upon to serve in the military. In addition, they were expected to help with public works projects, such as canal building or other favors their lords might ask. They might also be called upon to help at temples during the holy festivals or to clean or refurbish statues.

Clothing

The people wore a sampot, a rectangular cloth worn on the lower body. It was wrapped between the legs and secured with a belt at the back. The material would be simple for the peasants, but the upper classes wore elaborately decorated sampots. Men and women also wore a krama, which has a variety of uses, such as a scarf or bandanna. It can even be used as a hammock for small children.

The Khmers originated the belief that a person's soul resided in their heads, which is something Cambodians still practice to this day. Thus, it is taboo to touch or point with one's feet, especially toward another person. The feet are the lowest part of the body and are thought to be impure, making such a gesture an insult.

## Events of the 13th Century

Jayavarman VII died in 1218 and was succeeded by his son, Indravarman II. Like his father, Indravarman II was a Mahayana Buddhist. However, unlike his father, he wasn't skilled in military matters, and he lost control of some of the Champa territories, thus shrinking the size of Kambuja (Cambodia). In 1238, subjects within his kingdom rebelled under Si Inthrathit. He established his own kingdom, which was rather short-lived, as it ended in 1270. Si Inthrathit is often regarded as the ruler who freed Siam (modern-day Thailand) from Cambodian rule.

Indravarman II died in 1243 and was succeeded by Jayavarman VIII. Jayavarman, unlike his predecessors, was a follower of Shaivism. Jayavarman VIII aggressively opposed Buddhism and converted many Buddhist temples to Hindu ones. He systematically went on a destructive spree, defacing Buddhist images and destroying statues.

Between the 1270s and the 1290s, Kublai Khan of the massive Yuan Empire in China engaged in a military campaign in Southeast Asia, attacking kingdoms such as Burma, Vietnam, and Java. Burma was the only spot where the Mongols had any success, but many states agreed to pay tribute to avoid bloodshed. Kublai Khan even threatened the stability of Cambodia, attacking the Khmer Empire in

1283. In exchange for peace, Jayavarman VIII paid Kublai Khan tribute, which included elephant tusks, gold, and other precious items.

Jayavarman VIII was deposed by his son-in-law, Indravarman III, in 1295. King Indravarman III reigned from 1295 until 1308. The wandering Chinese diplomat Zhou Daguan, from whom we get much information about the Khmer Empire, related a curious story about Indravarman. Zhou says that when his father-in-law, Jayavarman VIII, had died, Indravarman III's wife stole his gold sword and gave it to Indravarman. It was said that was the reason why Jayavarman VIII's own son didn't succeed to the throne. Zhou also embroidered on the legend, saying, "The new king had a sacred piece of iron embedded in his body, so that if anything like a knife or an arrow touched him, he could not be injured."

Indravarman's procession when he became king was like those of the older days—replete in magnificence and glory and drawing great crowds. According to Zhou's accounts:

> Each time he came out, all his soldiers were gathered in front of him, with people bearing banners, musicians and drummers following behind him. One contingent was made up of three to five hundred women of the palace. They wore clothes with a floral design and flowers in their coiled-up hair, and carried huge candles, alight even though it was daylight...All the ministers, officials and relatives of the king were in front, riding elephants...Late came the king, standing on an elephant, the gold sword in his hand and the trunks of his elephant encased in gold.

Cambodia shifted away from the intolerance of his predecessor, Jayavarman VIII. Indravarman III followed Theravada Buddhism, which he made the state religion. Theravada Buddhism promotes more conservative beliefs. The focus is placed upon doctrine, rules of behavior, and the discourses and sermons of the Buddha. Followers are expected to meditate daily in order to free themselves from the attachments of the flesh, as that is the path to enlightenment.

The Theravada monks looked different too. According to Zhou Daguan's description in his book, *Customs of Cambodia*, he said that Theravada monks "shave their heads and dress in yellow. They leave their right shoulder uncovered, and wrap themselves in a robe made of yellow cloth and go barefoot." People were expected to support the monks by providing food, supplies, and medicine to them.

<u>Local Marketing</u>

Zhou Daguan presented a detailed description of the rural marketing practices in Cambodia, and historians have noted that they weren't much unlike Cambodian markets today. Zhou said that it was mostly conducted by women. The markets were open from early in the morning until mid-day. They didn't have stalls; instead, they simply unrolled mats on the ground. Like today's local markets, Zhou speculated that fees were charged to rent each space. They sold ivory, rhinoceros' horns for lowering fevers, lacquer, beeswax, and cardamom. Imported goods were also sold and consisted of metal goods, silk, porcelain, paper, and wicker.

**The Decline of Khmer**

Numerous factors fed into the decline of the Khmer Empire, which began its downfall slowly over the 13th century. The state's conversion from Hinduism to Mahayana Buddhism to Theravada Buddhism changed social and government systems. Over time, kings and the Hindu priests (brahmans) began to diminish in terms of importance; for example, kings lost their standing as being divinely chosen. Therefore, there was no need to erect more shrines, statues, or temples in their honor. The change in ideology also contributed to the lack of attention to infrastructure. Throughout the years, the Cambodian water management system began to fall into disrepair, as it hadn't been maintained. Therefore, floods and droughts were frequent, leading to crop failures.

The last Khmer king to have been mentioned in the monument inscriptions was Jayavarman IX, whose reign started in 1327, but others succeeded him, as the Khmer Empire didn't end until 1431. Jayavarman was a devoted Hindu, and he was assassinated in 1336 by the head of the royal gardens, whom historians assume took the throne, although it is very likely this story is simply legend and not fact.

### Foreign Relations

Between 1371 and 1432, twenty-one tributary missions were sent from Cambodia to the Ming court. This wasn't the first time missions had been sent to China from Khmer, but this number eclipsed those from previous years. The Cambodians were most eager to expand and exploit trade relations but were hampered by competition with the up-and-coming Ayutthaya Kingdom, which was centered in modern-day Thailand.

Around 1352, the Ayutthaya Kingdom invaded Khmer and replaced their rulers with Siamese kings. In 1357, Suryavamsa Rajadhiraja regained his throne, but he lost it again in 1393. When the Siam king, who also ruled the Khmer Empire, was assassinated, Ponhea Yat took his rightful place on the throne in Angkor.

However, Angkor was no longer a powerful city. The war with Ayutthaya had devastated the region. And not only that, but the government had failed to maintain the Cambodian hydraulic systems around Angkor. There are many other theories regarding the fall of Angkor, such as natural disasters, disease, and the decline of the royal cult. It is possible many of these factors played a role. Regardless, in 1431, Ponhea Yat moved the capital of Cambodia to the city of Phnom Penh. At Phnom Penh, the confluence of the Mekong River, the Tonle Sap, and the Bassac River served to stimulate trade. Phnom Penh was a fortified city, which allowed vigorous trade to occur. Pottery, fish, and fish sauce were exchanged for Chinese goods.

Around this time, a legend arose regarding the importance of Phnom Penh to explain this shift of control. It was said that an old woman discovered a Buddha image miraculously floating downstream to Phnom Penh. Historians consider the move to Phnom Penh the end of the Khmer Empire. It was replaced by a rather weak Khmer kingdom.

## The Longvek Era

Ang Chan was perhaps the best-known post-Angkor king. He was the viceroy and heir apparent of Phnom Penh, and in 1512, he came into conflict with a man named Sdach Korn. Sdach Korn killed the reigning king and drove Ang Chan out of the capital. Ang Chan fled to Siam and returned with a Siamese army in 1516, determined to expel the pretender. Sdach Korn retreated, and Ang took his rightful place on the throne. However, Sdach had not given his crown up, as he continued to label himself as the king. Fortunately, Ang was able to obtain firearms and cannons during the civil war. Around 1528 (possibly 1529), he captured Sdach Korn and beheaded him. That same year, he established the capital in the city of Longvek, which was on the banks of the Tonle Sap.

Ang Chan, who would rule until 1566, most likely made this move for a number of reasons. One of the major reasons was the devastation of the Khmer territory over the years. The Kingdom of Siam had made many incursions throughout the 14th century, and moving the capital to Longvek was smart military-wise, as it had a more defensible terrain. In addition, Longvek was located on the banks of the Tonle Sap, giving the Cambodians at least some limited access to trade networks. The historians of the time said, "Even though they appeared to have a secondary role in the Asian commercial sphere in the 16th century, the Cambodian ports did indeed thrive." Cambodians traded metals, silk, ivory, incense, and the like. The tributaries that were still accessible provided trading opportunities with the Chinese, Arabs, Indonesians, and Malays. Not only were those markets now open, but Europeans also traveled to the area, coming from Spain, the Netherlands, England, and Portugal.

The *Cambodian Royal Chronicles* and the *Royal Chronicles of Ayutthaya* record the numerous military clashes between the two nations, but modern historians, such as David Chandler and Michael Vickery, doubt the accuracy of these documents. What's more, Chandler states that the "least-recorded period of Cambodian history falls between Zhou Daguan's visit to Angkor [at the end of the $13^{th}$ century] and the restoration of some of the temples there by a Cambodian king named Chan in the 1550s and 1560s." This is why historians refer to this period, particularly between the $15^{th}$ and $16^{th}$ centuries, as Cambodia's "Dark Age," as there is little information about the history of Cambodia available. Although sources become a bit more frequent after the $16^{th}$ century, there still isn't enough to get a full picture of the rulers and their reigns. This lasts up until 1863, which was the beginning of the French protectorate of Cambodia.

### Ecological/Epidemiological Threats

During the Longvek era, the Khmer Empire was in decline. Archaeologists have noted multiple reasons why records were sparse, including the ever-present skirmishes, both from within and from without. Other reasons we haven't touched much upon were severe ecological disasters and the black plague.

Scientists theorized that the Black Death first appeared in Cambodia between 1330 and 1345, and the disease was most likely present for a time, with cases popping up even after the first major influx. Besides the Black Death, the excessive waters in the region traditionally give rise to malaria. This would more easily spread due to the poor water management system, as they weren't maintained, and stagnant water causes an increase in malaria-ridden mosquitoes.

When the population of the Khmer kingdom increased, a great strain was placed on the irrigation system, which was compounded by severe droughts alternated with excessive flooding. In addition, the people cut down more trees to create new rice paddies. Without the trees to absorb rainwater, the runoff carried silt downhill, filling up the canals the people used for transportation.

### The Continued Rise of the Ayutthaya Kingdom

As the Khmers declined, the Ayutthaya Kingdom (modern-day Thailand) expanded and became a major power in Southeast Asia. In 1568, the Siamese attacked Burma, seeking to annex their lands. However, Burma was victorious, and Ayutthaya became a vassal state. Ayutthaya attempted several times to free itself from Burmese vassalage, but it wouldn't be successful until 1584. Naresuan, one of Thailand's most beloved monarchs, participated in the battle for independence, becoming king in 1590 and ushering in a new age of expansion, one that put Cambodia in its crosshairs

### Legend of the Siamese-Cambodian War

Much of history is told in stories and legends, and Cambodia has a rather interesting one about the war with Ayutthaya. It tells the story of two brothers, Preah Ko and Preah Keo. Preah Ko, an ox who was birthed by a human mother, had divine powers and carried precious items in his belly.

As the legend relates, the king of Siam challenges the king of Cambodia, with Preah Ko involving himself to aid his king. The king of Siam is angered by this and sends an army to capture the two brothers. They flee to Longvek ("Lovek" in some records), where they hide in a thick bamboo forest. As the story goes, the king of Siam orders his men to fire silver coins into the bamboo forest. The local people rush in to snatch up the coins, obliterating the forest in the process. The brothers manage to flee once more, but in the end, the king of Siam captures them.

The forest in the legend relates to the Ranam forest, which played a part in the Siamese-Cambodian War.

### The Siamese-Cambodian War

In 1591, under General Phra Ratcha Manoo, Siam invaded Cambodia. King Satha I of Cambodia and his men were initially successful at the Ranam forest. However, Siamese reinforcements arrived, pushing the Cambodians out. Soon after, the Longvek citadel was besieged, but after three months, the Siamese were compelled to retreat.

In 1593, King Naresuan of Ayutthaya prepared a fresh assault on Cambodia after dealing with Burma. He divided his forces into four, and they all met to take down Longvek. By January 1594, the armies had met up, and they stormed the city. King Satha fled to Laos, but most of the Cambodian royal family were held as hostages and relocated to Siam (the Ayutthaya Kingdom). While there, they were kept under Siamese influence and control.

### The Cambodian-Spanish War

The Spanish had been on decent terms with King Satha I. However, despite the friendly overtures, they couldn't pass up the opportunity to expand their reach. Spain was very invested in spreading Christianity in Southeast Asia, and by gaining the stronghold of Cambodia, they would have an excellent launching-off point to do so. In 1593, Spain sent out an expedition to place a king on the throne who would align with their interests. Although they didn't prevail in the long run, they were able to establish a new king, Ponhea Ton, in 1597. He granted the Spanish the rights to two provinces on the east and west sides of the Mekong River.

Unfortunately, the Spanish were used to more brutal methods to spread Christianity, and Spanish, Portuguese, and Filipino fighters brutally attacked some Malay residences in the area. The Chams, Muslim Malays, and Cambodians retaliated to this move by massacring the Spanish, Portuguese, and Filipinos.

By 1599, Cambodia came under the control of the Ayutthaya Kingdom.

## New Capital

The capital of Cambodia moved several times during the post-Angkor period. Besides the already mentioned moves, later ones came during the 1590s and early 1600s, after the Siamese had made their move on Longvek. In the end, the capital was moved to Oudong.

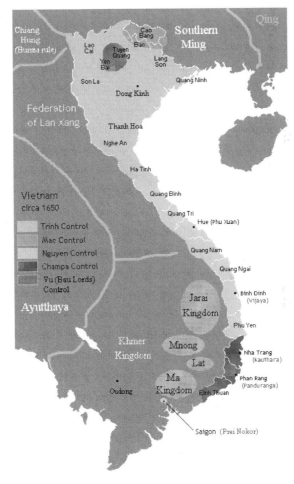

Cambodia (Khmer Kingdom) 1650

*https://commons.wikimedia.org/wiki/File:Vietnam1650.GIF*

# Chapter 4 – Colonial Period

Between the 17$^{th}$ and 18$^{th}$ centuries, Cambodia suffered a decline in its economy, as it had lost much of its coastland. Chinese traders, for the most part, bypassed them. By then, their main products to trade were brown sugar of poor quality, lacquer, and deer hides. One of those traders wrote, "Cambodia is a poor country with a poorly organized government and armed forces. There are no rich people."

To maintain a balance of power to contain the Siamese, whose power base was spreading, the king of Cambodia, Chey Chettha II (r. 1618-1628), married into the Nguyen family of Vietnam. He granted the Vietnamese settlements in Prey Nokor (modern-day Ho Chi Minh City). They established a customs house in Prey Nokor, which they used for trading purposes and to collect taxes. That was the start of a wave of Vietnamese immigrants into Cambodia. By the 1690s, Cambodia, which had never really recovered from its war with Ayutthaya, was forced to give the Mekong Delta area to Vietnam. In 1620, the Dutch East India Company also established relations with Cambodia, building an outpost at Kompong Luong, a port near Oudong, three years later.

## The Vietnamese and Thai People in Cambodia

In 1636, the more powerful members of the Nguyen dynasty of southern Vietnam split off from the Nguyen overlords in northern Vietnam, annexing areas in the southern Indochinese Peninsula. That cut off Cambodia's southern access to the sea and the Mekong River, affecting their trade. To exacerbate matters, many of the Cambodian ports along the Gulf of Siam were occupied by Sino-Vietnamese troops and private Vietnamese entrepreneurs. Cambodians who lived within those areas were cut off from the rest of Cambodia. That aroused a lot of resentment and anti-Vietnamese feelings. Additionally, it caused a lot of the elite and royal Cambodians who lived there to polarize along pro-Thai and pro-Vietnamese lines. It affected support for the candidates for Cambodian kingship, as their followers would choose kings based upon their support of either Siam or Vietnam.

The severe weakening of Cambodia left a power vacuum in the Mekong Delta. Thus, the Kingdom of Siam (modern-day Thailand) engaged in a power struggle with the Rattanakosin Kingdom of Dai Viet (modern-day Vietnam). The Cambodian kings became puppet kings of the two kingdoms, with a number of conflicts occurring on Cambodian soil. For instance, in 1717, Siam invaded Cambodia to help a sympathetic king regain the throne. Ultimately, Siam won, as the Vietnamese-aligned king switched sides, causing Vietnam to lose the suzerainty of Cambodia.

This polarization tended to weaken the Cambodian royalty in terms of focusing its attention on threats from foreign nations. As a result, in the 1750 and 1760s, there were a series of coups and countercoups by royal rivals.

In 1767, the Kingdom of Ayutthaya was conquered by Burma. A Thai overlord named Taksin set up his own kingdom. He wanted Cambodia to pay him tribute, which they rejected, insulting his honor in the process. King Outey II of Cambodia called Taksin the "son of a Chinese merchant and a commoner." In 1769, partly to uphold his honor and partly to put a new king on the throne, Taksin invaded Cambodia. While he managed to put Ang Non II on the throne, his efforts largely failed.

In 1772, the Tay Son rebellion broke out in Vietnam. This was led by the Tay Son brothers: Nguyen Hue, Nguyen Nhac, and Nguyen Lu. The Siamese sensed an opportunity and decided to push their way into the struggling country. On their way, the Siamese marched through Angkor and sent their navy out on several expeditions, destroying several small ports along the Gulf of Siam. They even burned down Phnom Penh. Just seven years later, the Thai placed seven-year-old Prince Ang Eng on the Cambodian throne under the regency of a pro-Thai official.

In 1782, Taksin was deposed and replaced by the Siamese minister of war, who was campaigning in Cambodia. That same year, Ang Eng had to flee to Siam due to Cham invasions. There was no immediate successor to the throne. Instead, a Cambodian official, Phraya Yommarat (Baen), became the regent, working closely with Siam in the process.

Ang Eng was adopted by Rama I, the Siamese minister of war who took over after Taksin. Eventually, Ang Eng would move back to Cambodia, taking the throne again in 1794. However, not everyone was happy with this move, as they enjoyed Baen as king. To prevent a civil war from breaking out, Rama I ordered Baen to leave Oudong, giving him the governorship of Battambang and Siem Reap instead. In 1796, Ang Eng died, and his five-year-old son, Ang Chan II, succeeded him.

### The Culture of 17th- & 18th-Century Cambodia: Study of the *Ramayana*

The Cambodians had seen much grief, but they kept their heritage and legacy alive despite the many wars.

The *Ramayana* is an old Sanskrit epic, cherished and performed in dance by the Cambodians. It was an escape and an inspiration to them; it was a means by which they kept their heritage alive. It is shared by the people of Thailand, Malaysia, Sri Lanka, and other Southeast Asian countries. Little is known about its author, Valmiki. The epic was written in India and describes the concept of a god who has taken a human form. The hero, Rama, must fight to win back his love, Sita, who was kidnapped by a demon.

Throughout the poem, Rama's virtues and strengths are extolled, and he is portrayed as being a model for rightful living. The quotes from *Ramayana* serve to inspire its readers with courage and love. For example, Rama says, "We have no right to ask when a sorrow comes, 'Why did this happen to me?' unless we ask the same question for every joy that comes our way."

Rama with Sita and his brother, Lakshmana, in the forest

*https://commons.wikimedia.org/wiki/File:Indischer_Maler_von_1780_001.jpg*

## The Shy King

Although Ang Chan II was the king of Cambodia, he wasn't allowed to enter the country until he came of age in 1806, remaining in Siam in the meantime. He had to struggle against his two brothers, Ang Em and Ang Snguon, and was forced to pay tribute to Vietnam as well. The Siamese demanded that Ang Chan appoint his two brothers as co-regents or viceroys, but Ang Chan refused. In 1811, with the help of the Siamese, Ang Snguon overthrew his brother and took the throne. Ang Chan fled to Vietnam, and in 1813, the Vietnamese returned to put him back in power, capturing the capital city of Oudong in the process. Ang Em and Ang Snguon fled to Bangkok. Ang Chan II then built two castles for himself—one at Phnom Penh and another at Lvea Aem—the latter of which stationed the bulk of his army. One thousand soldiers were assigned to protect King Ang Chan in Phnom Penh.

During his second reign, Cambodia was a vassal state of Vietnam and Siam. Emperor Gia Long of Vietnam said, "Cambodia is a small country, and we should maintain it as a child. We will be its mother, its father will be Siam."

It seems that Ang Chan II was rarely quoted, and none of his writings have survived. He was, in essence, an actor without lines. Ang Chan was timid, which would account for his silence in the annals. It was said of him that "a fresh wind or the cry of a bird could make him flee." A Vietnamese text states that Ang Chan was ill much of the time, which also might explain his silence.

## The Siamese-Vietnamese War of 1831–1834

Cambodia was stuck between two great forces: Thailand and Vietnam. And although things had remained somewhat civil, that situation couldn't last forever. Cambodia had control of the Mekong Delta, which granted it the commerce that ensued from maritime trade. In 1832, under General Bodindecha, the Siamese attempted to conquer the southern area of Vietnam, along with Cambodia as well.

The Cambodian king fled the capital, heading toward Vietnam for safety. For the Siamese troops to reach the capital of Vietnam, they had to proceed along the Bassac River toward the Mekong Delta. At the Vam Nao Canal, located between the Hau and the Tien Rivers, the Siamese and Vietnamese fleets met in early 1833. Initially, the Siamese ships prevailed, but the Vietnamese launched a massive counterattack on land. Bodindecha then disembarked his troops. The Siamese soon retreated, as did the Vietnamese.

The Siamese then moved toward the Vinh Te Canal. However, it was too shallow there, so they tried to have the galleys hauled by elephants to Kampot, a city in Cambodia. However, the Cambodian locals revolted and killed the elephant handlers, taking the elephants for themselves and pulling back. In the meantime, the Vietnamese kept attacking the Siamese forces. General Bodindecha told the two Cambodian princes, Ang Em and Ang Snguon, to burn Phnom Penh and take the inhabitants to the city of Battambang. However, the Cambodians rebelled, forcing the Siamese and the two princes to retreat to Siam.

The Siamese attempted again to take over the Cambodian communities controlled by the Vietnamese. Unfortunately for them, they lost, although Battambang remained under the control of Siam. At the end of the war, the Cambodian countryside was devastated, and the Vietnamese controlled most of territorial Cambodia.

### Royal Succession

Because the Cambodians had been able to preserve their culture, Emperor Minh Mang of Vietnam appointed General Truong Minh Giang to "Vietnamize" Cambodia. Vietnam wanted the Cambodians to serve in the Vietnamese military, and they also wanted to "reform" their habits, which they considered barbaric. The emperor said, "The barbarians [Cambodians] have become my children now...The people have no knowledge of [advanced] agriculture, using picks and hoes, rather than oxen. They grow enough rice for two meals a day, but they don't store any surplus."

The Vietnamese complained that the Cambodians wore robes without slits up the sides and ate with their fingers. However, the Cambodians resented these policies, and there were minor revolts against the Vietnamese, which began to break out in 1836 and occurred off and on through the years.

In 1835, Queen Ang Mey succeeded the throne. She wasn't the eldest daughter of Ang Chan, but she was preferred by the Vietnamese who installed her. In 1840, her older sister, Princess Baen, attempted to escape to Battambang. She was arrested, along with Queen Ang Mey and their other sisters, and they were later deported to Vietnam. Princess Baen was drowned, possibly being tortured beforehand. Unrest ensued, not just because of her death but also because their queen had been removed. According to one Vietnamese report, "The rebels have established posts along the riverbanks at strategic points. They appear and disappear at will. If our troops look to the east, the rebels escape to the west...They concentrate their forces where the jungle is thick, and in swampy areas where our troops cannot maneuver." Siam snatched the opportunity to invade Cambodia and install a puppet ruler. To help counter the rebellion so they could focus their efforts on Siam, Vietnam reinstated Queen Mey for a brief time. However, Ang Duong claimed he had the right to the throne, and since he was backed by Siam, he posed a great threat to Ang Mey. He was the son of the former king, Ang Eng, who ruled in the late $18^{th}$ century.

## The Siamese-Vietnamese War of 1841-1845

Prince Ang Duong supported Siam against Vietnam as the two countries sought to establish dominance over Cambodia. The military campaigns started when General Bodindecha, who had led the Siamese in the previous war, lay siege to Pursat, a Cambodian community controlled by Vietnam. He was able to establish a peaceful surrender there. Soon after, Emperor Minh Mang of Vietnam had a fatal accident, and the new Vietnamese emperor, Thieu Tri, decided to order a retreat instead of engaging the Siamese.

He had his forces retreat to An Giang Province in the Mekong Delta by that October. In the meantime, Vietnam had taken Cambodian Prince Ang Em to rally the Cambodians for the Vietnamese cause. However, the Siamese aided Ang Duong in gaining the throne, killing those Vietnamese they came across while doing so. The Siamese continued to establish their control and remove Vietnamese influence throughout the rest of 1841.

Between 1842 and 1843, disease and famine raged throughout Cambodia, and the fighting essentially ceased during that time. Cambodia was badly damaged due to these conflicts, and they began to argue amongst themselves, saying that they should switch sides and align with Vietnam. In 1845, Ang Duong had the Vietnamese sympathizers executed. After this, the armies began to make major moves again. A Vietnamese offensive occurred, forcing Bodindecha to march and defend Oudong. After the Siamese and Vietnamese engaged in minor battles to the north and south of Oudong, they decided to negotiate.

It took Ang Duong a bit of time to come around to accepting Vietnamese suzerainty, but he eventually did, allowing an agreement to be reached in 1847. This agreement gave both Siam and Vietnam joint domination over Cambodia, and Ang Duong had to send tribute to both Vietnam and Siam.

### The French Protectorate

Cambodia was at peace during the rest of King Ang Duong's reign, but it was a tenuous one. Ang Duong secretly yearned for a future in which the Cambodian people would no longer be involved in these wars. Cambodia needed a stronger power, one who could keep their perennial enemies at bay. Therefore, Ang negotiated with Emperor Napoleon III to get French protection for his country. His successor, King Norodom Prohmbarirak, followed up with the French. In 1862, France established a colony in Cochinchina (modern-day Vietnam), and the governor of Cochinchina realized that in order to expand their power, they needed Cambodia, which helped push the negotiations along. In 1863, France established Cambodia as a protectorate, allowing the monarchy to remain but taking most of the power (such as trade and foreign relations) for itself. Phnom Penh was the center of power, becoming the capital of Cambodia in 1866.

Under the treaty King Norodom signed, France agreed to offer Cambodia protection in exchange for timber concessions and mineral exploration rights. King Norodom was permitted to remain at the royal residence of Phnom Penh, but power was mostly invested in the hands of the French governor-general. In time, Siam agreed to this move, as it was granted the continued control of the city of Angkor and the new control over the province of Battambang. In 1887, since Cambodia was a part of the greater French Indochina, the governor-general ruled from the city of Saigon and later moved to Hanoi, which are both located in Vietnam. A resident-general was also appointed, and he was assisted by the local governors in Cambodia. Occasional revolts broke out against the king's acquiescence to French rule, but they were put down quickly by the French government.

The French also wanted Norodom to help pay the costs of the French protectorate through taxes on the sale of opium and liquor. In the 1880s, the French tightened their control on the Cambodian court, as they wanted Cambodia to change some of its traditional customs and to gain a firmer grip on its economy, but the Cambodians resisted.

Norodom assigned his son, also named Norodom, to be his heir apparent. However, he got into a disagreement with the French, and when King Norodom passed in 1904, the throne went to his half-brother, Sisowath, instead. Sisowath supported the French, and they paid him in kind, building him a new palace and granting him a huge ration of opium each year.

Since the French brought in reforms, such as reducing the king's powers and the abolition of slavery, the king became a mere figurehead.

## Cambodian Revolt

Not every Cambodian agreed with these French actions, as they saw the French as invading and imposing their own ideas onto them. In 1885, before Norodom's death, some Cambodians revolted under Norodom's other half-brother, Si Votha. The French refused to help initially, as they saw this as perfect leverage to get Norodom to sign new reforms. Eventually, Norodom signed, and the French helped quell the rebellion.

## Reorganization of the Government

In 1896, Great Britain, which controlled nearby Burma and British Malay, and France signed a sphere of influence agreement regarding the Indochinese Peninsula, especially the Kingdom of Siam. Under that agreement, Siam ceded Battambang back to Cambodia.

Although the Cambodian sovereignty itself was left intact, the French gained even more control. Cambodia was considered a revenue-producing country. However, corruption was rampant, and banditry was common. Although the Cambodians paid high taxes, the tax rolls were misrepresented, and rice harvests were underestimated. French officials were paid high salaries while the people had trouble making ends meet. Of course, this only added to the resentment Cambodians felt toward the French.

## Economy

Cambodia paid higher taxes than the other French Southeast Asian colonies. Their economy was built on rice and peppers. When French investors came in, they created an automobile industry. Minority groups handled industrial and commercial work. Some were immigrants from Champa. The Kui (or Kuy) people from modern-day Thailand and Laos smelted iron ore in the north. Rural trade was operated by the barter system, and an important railway was built, connecting Phnom Penh and Battambang on the Siamese border.

Under the French, more modern agricultural techniques were introduced, and colonial entrepreneurs were granted concessions in Battambang Province. Cotton and corn were also raised. Rubber plantations were established and headed by French investors. However, the jobs at those plantations were given to the Vietnamese instead of to the Cambodians. Discrimination was practiced against the Cambodians, which prevented them from holding higher-level positions. Those were reserved for the French.

# Chapter 5 – War and Politics

### The 1916 Protests

Cambodia did not play a direct role in World War I, which lasted from 1914 to 1918. However, they did play an indirect part, as France used their Southeast Asian territories to help fund the war efforts. In late 1915, 300 peasants who worked near Phnom Penh met with King Sisowath to ask for a reduction in taxes, adding that they wanted the taxes to be collected by Cambodians, not French officials. Sisowath gave them only nominal acknowledgment. More and more people joined and marched to the palace. French police estimated that thousands participated, and the French who resided there also reported violence.

The gap between the income of the Cambodians and the French officials was wide. The Chinese merchants, too, benefited from the profits of Cambodia. The protests subsided somewhat when the Cambodian king toured the provinces and calmed the people. Between 1918 and 1919, there were very poor harvests and even famine throughout the countryside. Despite that, French officials and Chinese merchants continued to make a profit. Medical services were very poor, and electricity and running water were almost unknown outside of Phnom Penh.

## The Assassination of the Resident-General

Felix Louis Bardez was the resident-general of Cambodia in 1923. He was very ambitious, and he noted that tax revenues were successively falling, so he reorganized the system of tax collection and supervised it directly at times. Bardez was eager to find instances in which books were doctored and compromises had been made to the tax collection procedures.

Once his activity was noted by his superiors, he was transferred to another province where tax revenues had been less than expected. As soon as he arrived, a new tax was imposed upon the people to pay for the construction of a mountain resort for French officials. When a Cambodian official tried to collect the taxes in 1925, he was severely beaten by the villagers.

During the same year, Bardez, along with his interpreter and Cambodian militiamen, visited a village where there were delinquent taxpayers. The entourage was attacked by about thirty people, and Bardez and his interpreter were beaten to death. Their bodies were then mutilated.

Crowds began to gather, mainly those who had come to hear the resident-general speak. They staged a march, demanding a remission in their taxes, but they were suppressed when more troops arrived and dispersed the crowd.

A trial was held in Phnom Penh, but high-ranking officials tried to block evidence that the Cambodians paid very high taxes per capita. French officials interfered with the defense counsel; for instance, the defense counsel's tea was poisoned, and the court stenographer was transferred to another district. Over 200 people were questioned. In the end, the prime suspect, Neou, was shot when he resisted arrest, and Chuon, his partner, was condemned to death, but only after much time had passed. The defense took the position that the whole village was at fault, as they had been provoked by an unjust system and the extreme behavior of Resident-General Bardez, who, among other things, refused the prisoners their request to have lunch the day he died.

After the trial, a royal ordinance was passed, declaring the entire village was guilty.

### Internal Improvements

Between 1928 and 1932, a railroad was built in Cambodia, which boosted Chinese and Vietnamese immigration. The Vietnamese sought employment in the urban sector, allowing the cities to grow.

The Great Depression hit Cambodia, as well as much of the world, during the 1930s, and the price of rice plummeted. Tax collection likewise fell. At the end of the Depression, the growth of maize increased substantially.

In 1939, Siam was renamed "Thailand" and took over a segment in northwestern Cambodia a few years later. They opposed the return of the French and formed several independence movements. One such group called themselves the Khmer Issarak, which means "Free Khmer," which would play an important role in Cambodian history after World War II ended.

### World War II

In 1941, a year after France fell to the Germans in World War II, the Imperial Japanese Army entered Cambodia. They set up garrisons there but still allowed the French officials to remain. At this time, France was operating under Vichy France, which was essentially controlled by the Axis Powers. In 1945, a year after France was liberated, Japan overthrew the French rule in Indochina. The Japanese encouraged the current king of Cambodia, Norodom Sihanouk, to proclaim independence. Instead of naming his kingdom after Cambodia, he instead called it "Kampuchea." Japan immediately ratified Cambodian independence, establishing a consulate in the capital. In exchange, Sihanouk got rid of the previous treaties made with France and created an alliance with Japan.

At the end of World War II, in August of 1945, Japan surrendered, and the Allied military entered Indochina. Son Ngoc Thanh, the former foreign minister, made himself the new prime minister. In October of that year, French authorities returned. They arrested Son Ngoc Thanh for collaborating with the Japanese and exiled him to France. Many of his supporters joined the Khmer Issarak, as they believed in Son Ngoc Thanh's vision of a government without colonial rule.

### Early Political Parties

In Phnom Penh, Norodom Sihanouk acted as the head of state and negotiated with France for independence while keeping an eye on the independence movements, which threatened to spill over into a civil war. In 1946, France allowed political parties to be formed in Cambodia and to begin drafting a constitution. These parties were the Democratic Party, led by Prince Sisowath Yuthevong, and the Liberal Party, headed by Prince Norodom Norindeth. Prince Yuthevong favored the kind of democracy practiced in France, which was preferred by the younger members of the bureaucracy. They were supporters of the Khmer Issarak movement as well. The short-lived Liberal Party was composed mostly of elderly members and landowners who wanted to preserve the status quo and slowly introduce democratic measures.

The Democrats gained the majority of seats in the Consultative Assembly, which would help guide the drafting of the new constitution, but they were fiercely opposed by Sihanouk. Sihanouk preferred the Liberal Party himself, as it would leave him with more power. Cambodia was also threatened by extremists in Vietnam, namely Ho Chi Minh and his followers, so Sihanouk didn't want to hastily expel the French. However, Sihanouk knew he was in a delicate position, as this was a tumultuous time. He realized angering the majority party wouldn't bode well for him in the long run. He agreed to the constitution, which reduced his role to that of a constitutional monarch. However, the document didn't define his role clearly, which he would later turn to his advantage.

## The First Indochina War (1946-1954)

In 1946, France engaged in a war to maintain its control over Indochina, which included Cambodia, Laos, and Vietnam. France was opposed by Vietnam, namely the Viet Minh, the umbrella organization of Ho Chi Minh; the Khmer Issarak, who had been occupying sectors in northwestern Cambodia; the Pathet Lao, a communist group in Laos; and the Lao Issara, a non-communist organization. French forces included troops from Cambodia, French-controlled Vietnam, and Laos, as well as mercenary troops from other French colonies.

While Cambodians fought in the war, most of the fighting took place in Vietnam. However, there were several events that took place that greatly impacted the country. In 1950, Son Ngoc Minh, the leader of the United Issarak Front, which was made up mostly of members from the recently formed Indochina Communist Party, declared Cambodia's independence, as his group controlled nearly one-third of the country. By 1954, it is assumed that the United Issarak Front controlled half of Cambodia.

In the meantime, King Sihanouk found the war to be the perfect opportunity to flex his power. In 1952, Sihanouk made a determined speech, saying, "All is disorder. Hierarchy no longer exists. There is no rational employment of talent." He then staged a coup of his own government to rid himself of the Cabinet, which was controlled by the Democrats. He hired Moroccan mercenaries to surround the National Assembly and dismissed the Democrats. Sihanouk suspended the constitution and made himself prime minister, promising to bring full independence to Cambodia in three years.

King Norodom Sihanouk

*https://commons.wikimedia.org/wiki/File:Norodom_Sihanouk_1941.jpg*

Leftist radical Cambodian students studying in France wrote a manifesto, calling for Sihanouk's abdication and accusing him of collaborating with the French. One of the major leaders of that group was Saloth Sar, also known as Pol Pot, who would become very influential in future Cambodian politics, to put it lightly.

In January of 1953, the National Assembly didn't pass Sihanouk's budget, and Sihanouk declared martial law, arresting some Democrat members in the process. He realized that with the tensions in the country, he needed to maintain a very firm grip on his power. He justified this move to a reporter, saying, "I am the natural ruler of the country...and my authority has never been questioned."

In February of 1953, Sihanouk traveled to France. He made contact with the elderly French president, Vincent Auriol, as Sihanouk wanted France to be a future ally after Cambodian independence, and he also wanted support against the machinations of the Communist Party of Kampuchea. However, Auriol was relatively powerless, and he also looked upon Sihanouk's appeal as alarming. Sihanouk then went to Canada and the United States to publicize Cambodia's difficulty in expelling the French.

By October of 1953, the French had granted Sihanouk authority over the armed forces, foreign affairs, and the judiciary system. On November 9th, 1953, Sihanouk delivered on his promise for full independence.

### End of French Colonial Rule

In 1953, the French colonial period ended, as Cambodia had gained its independence. The First Indochina War wouldn't end until the following year, and the casualties were devastating. It is estimated that around 134,500 French soldiers and their allies had died or been declared missing. The Viet Minh casualties are harder to estimate, as there are two figures for them. According to Western historians, between 175,000 and 300,000 Vietnamese died or went missing, while Vietnamese sources say it was closer to 191,000.

The war was settled with the Geneva Conference. That conference divided Vietnam into two sectors: North Vietnam, which would be controlled by the Viet Minh, and South Vietnam, which would be controlled by the dynastic Nguyen rule under Bao Dai until a democratic government could be established. Laos was also granted full independence, as was Cambodia. Sihanouk marched to Phnom Penh in triumph, becoming widely popular with the people.

### New Political Parties: 1955 Elections

This was the first election after the country's independence had been internationally recognized, and many different parties took part.

The Krom Pracheachon was founded in 1954, and it declared a socialist platform. Pol Pot was involved in its foundation, and it was essentially a front for the Communist Party of Kampuchea. It only received about 4 percent of the vote.

In 1955, Norodom Sihanouk suddenly abdicated in favor of his father, Norodom Suramarit. He then founded the Sangkum Reastr

Niyum (typically translated as the "People's Socialist Community"). As one might expect, it was a pro-Sihanouk party, advocating for a more conservative style of government. They did astoundingly well, earning almost 83 percent of the votes.

The Democratic Party was still around, but it had fewer members than before. Still, it did the second best in the election, winning 12 percent of the vote.

Prior to the 1955 general election, several newspapers that were critical of Sihanouk were shut down. Pracheachon candidates were harassed, and ballot boxes that most likely contained Democratic ballots disappeared. Sihanouk later admitted that fraud took place, mainly in areas where the Pracheachon would have done very well. Sihanouk's party would remain in power until 1970, dominating the political scene in Cambodia for fifteen years.

### Cambodia during the Vietnam War

During this time, the eastern sectors of Cambodia were havens for pro-Communist North Vietnamese army forces and the National Liberation Front, which was also pro-Communist. Domestic politics in Cambodia became polarized, and opposition to the Cambodian government grew. The clandestine Communist Party of Kampuchea, led mainly by Pol Pot, came out of hiding. Sihanouk called them the "Khmer Rouge," meaning "Red Khmers."

The Vietnam War, also known as the Second Indochina War, broke out in Vietnam in November of 1955, although conflicts in the country had been present long before then. Both sides wanted a unified Vietnam, but they wanted Vietnam to be united in their style of government and beliefs. The Viet Cong of North Vietnam initiated a guerrilla war in democratic South Vietnam, which was led by President Ngo Dinh Diem, whose primary ally was the United States, although other countries took part on both sides. Cambodia declared neutrality, but in time, the war would spill over, affecting other Southeast nations.

In the 1958 election, there were only two parties: Sihanouk's party, the Sangkum, and the Pracheachon. As for the latter party, all but one withdrew before the election due to police repression.

In April of 1960, Sihanouk's father died, and Sihanouk had himself declared "chief of state," while his mother, Queen Kossamak, served as a ceremonial monarch.

Toward the end of the 1960s, Cambodia's economy faltered. Much of the rice crop had been illegally sold to the North Vietnamese soldiers, so the Cambodian soldiers were ordered to confiscate it and store it in government warehouses. There was a low yield in the rice and cotton crops, which was compounded by the high interest charged on loans to farmers. That created unrest and triggered riots. In 1967, a full-scale revolt broke out in Battambang. Sihanouk was in France at that time, so his prime minister, Lon Nol, declared martial law. Supposedly, the national police were offered a bounty for each rebel or leftist head they sent to the capital. Even though this might be fiction, it does help to show how the people saw Lon Nol's methods, as they were incredibly harsh.

In 1968, Lon Nol resigned due to a car accident he had been in, although it is possible his actions played a part in his abrupt departure. Lon Nol would become the prime minister again in 1969. After Lon Nol left, Sihanouk appointed some leftists to government positions in a weak attempt to show some support of the leftist movement.

Rise of the Khmer Rouge

During the 1960s, the communist Khmer Rouge (CPK) created the Revolutionary gradually created an army, which later morphed into the Revolutionary Army of Kampuchea. However, the followers of the Khmer Rouge were small in number at this initial stage, numbering somewhere between 4,000 to 5,000 men, but they were fiercely nationalistic. They had no interest in aligning themselves with North Vietnam. When Sihanouk restored Lon Nol to power, Lon suggested that Sihanouk establish relations with the US, which he did.

## The Bombing Campaigns

Since the Viet Cong were harboring troops within twenty miles of the Cambodian-Vietnamese border, the United States initiated a bombing campaign called Operation Patio and Operation Menu against Viet Cong bases in eastern Cambodia in 1969 and 1970. The US backed that up with a ground offensive, which included both US and South Vietnamese troops. In 1970, US President Richard Nixon announced the entrance of American troops in Cambodia, only doing so after it had already occurred. Those campaigns were done in support of Lon Nol's Khmer National Armed Forces (FANK). Once the Americans and South Vietnamese left, the FANK was attacked by the Viet Cong and Khmer Rouge. Because of that, the US again resumed their attacks with Operation Freedom Deal, which will be covered in more depth in the next chapter.

Sihanouk publicly denounced the bombings, but it was revealed later by Peter Rodman, a US government official, that "Prince Sihanouk complained bitterly to us about these North Vietnamese bases in his country and invited us to attack them." US President Lyndon B. Johnson heard the same from his emissary to Cambodia in 1968.

To this day, historians argue whether or not the US actually received approval from Sihanouk. Either way, the damage had been done. In fact, one of the reasons for the rise of the Khmer Rouge was the extreme antipathy they had for the US because they had carried the Vietnam War into Cambodia. It caused a great deal of anti-Sihanouk feelings and resulted in a purge of moderates, even including moderate Communists.

# Chapter 6 – The Cambodian Civil War

## The Coup

During the late 1960s, Sihanouk discovered that Communist China was backing the Communist Party in Cambodia and threatened to close the Chinese embassy due to the Communist propaganda China was distributing. Zhou Enlai promised Sihanouk that all future material would be sent to Cambodia's information ministry first. It was a weak promise, but it calmed Sihanouk down enough, and he allowed the embassy to remain open.

In 1968, the Khmer Rouge launched their first assault, starting the Cambodian Civil War. This will be talked about more in the next section, but it is important to note here, as Cambodia was plagued by Khmer Rouge incursions on top of the following events.

Sihanouk built two casinos in 1969, and Cambodians, who were desperate for money, lost thousands of dollars at the gambling tables, leading to a higher rate of bankruptcies and suicides. In early 1970, Sihanouk went away on yet another trip to Europe. When he returned to his country, he would find it in utter chaos.

Sihanouk had been having medical issues toward the end of 1969, and he made Sisowath Sirik Matak his deputy prime minister. When he left that October to get treatment, Sirik Matak overstepped his boundaries, telling ambassadors to contact Lon Nol, the prime minister, instead of Sihanouk, as well as closing the casinos and privatizing the banks. When Sirik Matak went to Hanoi in North Vietnam in an effort to get them to close down their bases in Cambodia, he was horrified to find that Sihanouk had agreed to house those Communist bases inside Cambodian borders. Not only that, but Sihanouk had agreed to open the port of Sihanoukville (named after himself), which he used to ship in weapons for the Vietnam War. In exchange, Hanoi agreed to buy rice at inflated prices. The Cambodian economy was faltering at the time, so Sihanouk saw that as a benefit, but these activities were abhorrent to Sirik Matak.

In March of 1970, back in Cambodia, there were massive demonstrations in Phnom Penh against the North Vietnamese. The North Vietnamese and Viet Cong embassies in Cambodia were sacked. Lon Nol stepped in, closing the port at Sihanoukville to North Vietnam and demanding that all the Viet Cong who were present in the north of Cambodia leave by March 15th of that year. Predictably, that didn't happen. On the morning of March 16th, thousands of Cambodian youths gathered around the National Assembly, clamoring for action. That same day, the National Assembly was in session to consider corruption charges against Colonel Oum Mannorine, the Secretary of Defense and Sihanouk's brother-in-law. Sihanouk, in the meantime, had left Europe and headed to potential allies for more backing instead of heading home to quell the unrest.

According to Sihanouk, Oum Mannorine had done nothing wrong. He had heard word that Lon Nol and Sirik Matak were planning a coup and had attempted to arrest them. It is possible this was true, as Oum and all of Sihanouk's loyal security men were placed under house arrest. Siri Matak then finally persuaded Lon Nol to remove Sihanouk as prime minister. Even so, Lon Nol was very reluctant to do so, and allegedly, Sirik Matak had three armed soldiers stand by while Lon Nol signed the documents approving the coup.

On March 18th, the National Assembly met to argue the issue. Finally, all except one member of the Assembly voted to invoke Article 122 of the Cambodian constitution, which was the no-confidence vote. Lon Nol took over as acting prime minister. Although this was, in essence, a coup, it was done rather peacefully and according to the law rather than through assassinations and violence. It also set the stage for the future Khmer Republic.

Sihanouk's mother, Queen Kossamak, was asked to leave the palace. She did so, joining Sihanouk, who was, by that time, in Beijing—the heart of Communist China. In July, Lon Nol's government held a military trial and condemned Sihanouk of treason. They sentenced him to death in absentia.

Lon Nol, Future President of the Khmer Republic

*https://commons.wikimedia.org/wiki/File:LonNol.jpg*

While in China, Zhou Enlai assured Sihanouk that China still recognized him as the head of Cambodia. He promised military aid to fight against Lon Nol's newly formed Cambodian government. Sihanouk announced the formation of this resistance movement in March 1970, which he called the National United Front of Kampuchea (FUNK), and endorsed the Khmer Rouge, hoping their strong base in the country would fuel his return to the throne. Khmer soldiers approved of this, demonstrating in various parts of the country. In addition, Sihanouk made an impassioned announcement via Beijing Radio for Cambodians to rebel against the coup. His supporters violently revolted in various provinces and in Kompong Cham, a city in the Mekong Delta. Two deputy members of the National Assembly were killed. The demonstrations were crushed by the regular Cambodian army, which killed several hundred and arrested thousands.

In May, Sihanouk formed a government-in-exile based in Beijing, which he called the Royal Government of the National Union of Kampuchea (GRUNK). Numerous Communist countries sided with GRUNK, leaving Lon Nol in a rough spot. Sihanouk, who had spent the last few decades fighting the Communists, was now firmly on their side.

In October of 1970, Lon Nol formally established the Khmer Republic, with him remaining as prime minister. The US provided assistance to the new government's military forces. Lon Nol appealed to the United Nations to gain support for his new government while maintaining his neutrality in the Vietnam War. He denounced interference "by foreign forces, whatever camp they come from."

### The Cambodian Civil War (January 1968–April 1975)

In April of 1970, the United States and South Vietnam, in order to support their efforts in the Vietnam War, had initiated the Cambodian campaign with the aid of the Royal Cambodian Army. They started by dismantling a number of Vietnamese logistical installations in Cambodia, but many of those had already been relocated farther inland and escaped notice.

In March of 1970, the leader of the Khmer Rouge, Nuon Chea, asked that the North Vietnamese intercede and put a stop to the Cambodian army's efforts. Because of protests in America, the US pulled back their troops but still gave some support, although it was limited. Following that, the North Vietnamese attacked the Royal Cambodian Army and overtook most of northern Cambodia. Rather than rule the territory, they turned northern Cambodia over to the local Khmer Rouge.

### Operation Chenla I, August 1970–February 1971

The Khmer Republic attracted thousands of young and enthusiastic Cambodians to its ranks, eventually growing to number around 250,000 by 1975. These men, of course, were untrained. Experts have said that there was a great deal of corruption in the army, and very often, the numbers of active fighters were exaggerated. The system of food and supplies was haphazard, and it was suspected that much was sold on the black market and bypassed the troops. Hence, those who were genuinely fighting to preserve the Khmer Republic were frequently deprived of rations.

Operation Chenla I started off well, with the Khmer National Armed Forces (FANK) forces capturing their objectives without much trouble. However, in January of 1971, the People's Army of Vietnam (PAVN) and the Khmer Rouge attacked the airport in Phnom Penh and virtually destroyed the aircraft there. However, this was almost a blessing in disguise, as the planes were old, reconditioned Soviet airplanes, which the US then replaced with newer models. Regardless, this move essentially ended the operation.

## Operation Chenla II, August 1971–December 1971

The objective of this operation was to clear Route 6 and reopen communications with one of Cambodia's largest cities, Kompong Thon. In late August 1971, the FANK was able to capture the PAVN-held city of Barai. Heavy fighting occurred during the bloody advance on Phnom Santuk, but it was taken by September, along with the neighboring city of Tang Krasang. By late October, FANK declared the operation a success, although they hadn't truly secured the route, which proved problematic.

Soon after, the PAVN forces received reinforcements, forcing the FANK back. During the month of December alone, PAVN forces had wiped out as many as ten infantry battalions. It was a tremendous loss for the national troops.

## Operation Freedom Deal, May 1970–August 1973

After the US began gradually pulling troops out of Cambodia, US actions basically focused on removing enemy supply lines, which was the stated objective of Operation Freedom Deal. However, the US soon extended the operation so forces could engage in search-and-rescue missions to retrieve downed South Vietnamese pilots. And soon after that, the operation expanded its parameters once more.

In a last-ditch effort, especially seeing as the US had left the South Vietnamese and Cambodians to fend off the PAVN and Khmer Rouge on their own, the US restarted its aerial bombings in Cambodia. Most of the flights were in support of the FANK troops. However, US Ambassador Emory Swank later admitted that they often didn't know what villages were being bombed.

When Lon Nol announced a ceasefire after the Paris Peace Accords were signed, the US bombings stopped in hopes that unity could be achieved, but the Khmer Rouge continued the fight. The US resumed bombings later that year, forcing the Communists back. Operation Freedom Deal ended in August 1973, and overall, a large number of aerial strikes had hit villages or cities containing a large number of civilians. However, when looking at the final figures of the war's death count, it is hard to distinguish which ones were caused by the US bombing campaigns and which ones were a part of the greater Cambodian Civil War. Estimates are very wide, ranging from 30,000 to 500,000, with some scholars saying the US accounted for 50,000 to 150,000 deaths. The actual number will likely never be known for sure.

### The Paris Peace Accords, January 1973

On January 27th, 1973, the Paris Peace Accords were signed by the United States, North Vietnam, South Vietnam, and the provisional government in South Vietnam, which was operated by North Vietnam. The treaty stipulated that the US and its allies would withdraw from Vietnam within sixty days, prisoners of war would be returned, all foreign troops would be withdrawn from Cambodia, a ceasefire would take place in South Vietnam along specified borders, the US would oversee financial aid to all of Indochina, and a commission would be established to monitor these agreements.

A new constitution had been written a year before in April, with Lon Nol being elected as the president of the Khmer Republic soon after. It was said that the election was deliberately rigged. Political parties cropped up, as per the new constitution, but they provided no sense of unity to the country; instead, they just promoted factionalism.

This was the exact opposite of what Cambodia needed at the time, as it was already fractured. Since the Khmer Republic was so weak, the Khmer Rouge essentially controlled most of the country. Under them, religion was suppressed, and people were executed for disobeying orders or asking questions. It seems the Khmer Rouge began acting more violently toward the populace when PAVN forces began to refocus their efforts on South Vietnam. Since there was no one to police the Khmer Rouge, the members, which were led by Pol Pot, among others, could do as they wanted. As time passed, the Khmer Rouge cut ties with the North Vietnamese and Sihanouk, who had placed his bets on their alliance so he could regain the throne.

By 1975, the Khmer Republic was in shambles. Phnom Penh, which had around 600,000 people before the war, now had to accommodate two million people, mostly refugees. And when the Khmer Rouge gained control of the rivers, by which Phnom Penh mainly received supplies, it was truly the beginning of the end for the Cambodian capital.

### Operation Eagle Pull, April 12th, 1975

It was quite clear to those running the Khmer Republic that its days were numbered. The Khmer Rouge continued to close in, even hitting Pochentong, the airport in Phnom Penh to which the United States sent supplies, forcing the US to suspend air traffic. They lifted this suspension a day later, as the military realized Phnom Penh would be completely lost without their aid. Unfortunately, their aid would only continue for a short time. Soon, the Khmer Rouge overran the last positions the Khmer Republic held on the Mekong, allowing the Khmer Rouge to focus all its efforts on Phnom Penh. That same day, April 1st, 1975, Lon Nol resigned and went into exile. A military advisor said of Lon Nol's resignation, "He got us all to rise up and fight. Now he's deserting us."

The United States realized it had to evacuate its men, something they had been considering since 1973. According to that plan, there were three different options. But after hearing the predictions that there would be 3,600 evacuees, which was far more than the original 400 that had been planned, the United States realized they needed a different strategy. US Marines would secure the Phnom Penh airport while helicopters would airlift evacuees from Phnom Penh, then taking them to the airport. After the drop-off, the evacuees would be sent to Thailand.

The evacuation went smoothly, although there were fewer evacuees than had been anticipated. The top Cambodian officials were not among those evacuated, as they were upset that the Americans would no longer offer support. Sirik Matak notably remarked, "I have committed this mistake of believing in you, the Americans." The only exception was Saukham Khoy, the acting president of Cambodia.

Acting President Saukham Khoy Flees the Country

*https://commons.wikimedia.org/wiki/File:Saukham_Koy_arrives_on_USS_Okinawa.jpg*

## The Fall of Phnom Penh

After the evacuees had been airlifted from the city, a Supreme Committee was gathered to rule over what was left of the Khmer Republic. The next day, April 13th, 1975, the Khmer Rouge continued its assault on the capital. The Supreme Committee, which was headed by Lieutenant General Sak Sutsakhan, decided to send a peace offer to Sihanouk, in which they would transfer power over to him while making it clear they would not be surrendering to the Khmer Rouge.

The battle continued on April 14th. In the morning, two huge bombs, which were dropped by the Khmer Air Force, exploded near Sak's office, killing several officers and wounding around twenty others. That same day, Takhmau, the capital of the Kandal Province, which was just seven miles away from the capital, fell to the Khmer Rouge. The southern areas of Phnom Penh erupted into a fierce battle. On April 15th, with the Khmer Rouge pressing closer with every hour, Sak Sutsakhan tried unsuccessfully to make a peace offer with the Khmer Rouge, but it was ignored. On April 17th, the members of the Cabinet and the Supreme Committee realized they were only delaying fate. They decided to evacuate to the Thai border. Sak Sutsakhan and Long Boret, who had been instrumental behind the latest peace offer, remained in the capital, leaving on one of the last helicopters. Sak made it out, but Long was not so lucky. It is not known exactly what happened, but it is believed his helicopter didn't take off in time. The Khmer Rouge executed him that same day. As for Sirik Matak, he died a few days later, presumably by a firing squad.

The Khmer Rouge victoriously entered the city. They executed the remaining senior officials and FANK officers. Soon after taking the city, they told the residents of Phnom Penh that they had to evacuate because the US was going to bomb the city, telling them they could return in three days. However, this was not true, as the US had no intentions of engaging in such a campaign. The Khmer Rouge wanted to rid the city of the refugees, as they had fled from their advance, meaning they were not loyal to the cause. Over two million people were pushed out of the city, forced to march in the hot summer heat. At checkpoints, their belongings were searched, with Khmer Rouge officers confiscating whatever they wanted. It is believed 200,000 people died on this march.

# Chapter 7 – Democratic Kampuchea

"Democratic Kampuchea" was the term the Khmer Rouge gave Cambodia in January 1976. "Democratic" was a deliberate misnomer. This was a communist country. All the former traditional structures of the Cambodian governments of the past were abolished. As per the Marxist-Leninist structure, the nation was a one-party state, the Communist Party of Kampuchea, and it was headed by the Communist Party's secretary general, Pol Pot. Although it wasn't officially named Democratic Kampuchea until 1976, the new government went into existence starting in 1975 after the fall of Phnom Penh.

After the fall of the Cambodian capital, the former president, Norodom Sihanouk, was called in from China to act as the new head of state. He was paraded into Phnom Penh with great pomp and circumstance.

On January 5ᵗʰ, 1976, the Communist Party of Kampuchea (CPK) established a constitution. Assembly members would be elected by secret ballot. A State Praesidium (an executive council) was also created, with the Kampuchean People's Representative Assembly (KPRA) selecting members every five years. However, the members of the KPRA were never elected; instead, they were chosen by the CPK, which essentially held all the power in the country.

The transformation of the country took place in stages. During the first phase, and as mentioned above, forced migrations of people took place, as the Khmer Rouge sought to empty Phnom Penh of its native people who held different political views or of the Vietnamese who lived among them. The government would control their fates, at least for those who survived. For instance, those who had technical skills were sent back to the cities to aid in factory production. Most of the urban population would be sent to agricultural communes, working fields with little knowledge of agricultural practices. The Khmer Rouge wanted the Cambodians to produce three tons of rice per hectare, which was an incredible feat even with know-how. Of course, famine was unavoidable. And to make matters worse, the government saw acts like picking wild fruit as a crime punishable by death. Workers couldn't leave the communes and had to adhere to strict rules and backbreaking long hours. In addition, the government, wishing to stay away from Western influences, relied on traditional medicine, which only helped to aid in a greater number of deaths. During the Khmer Rouge regime, it is believed between 1.5 million to 2 million people died.

In February 1976, Sihanouk was taken around the countryside, and it is said he was "shocked" to observe the relocation of the population and the conditions under which they were living. After the tour, Sihanouk tendered his resignation, which was initially refused. However, by mid-April, they had accepted it, placing Sihanouk under house arrest at his palace in Phnom Penh. He would remain as a prisoner until 1979. It seems that the removal of Sihanouk was inevitable either way, though. Earlier that year, Zhou Enlai had died, leaving Sihanouk with no protector. A confidential document that came to light years later stated, "Sihanouk has run out of breath. He cannot go forward. Therefore we have decided to retire him."

Mao Zedong, the Communist Party Chairman in China, died in September of 1976. To keep up good relations, Pol Pot, who became the prime minister of Kampuchea the following month, planned to visit Mao's successor when he was voted in and installed.

### Organization and Administration

As mentioned above, all the power belonged to the Communist Party of Kampuchea (CPK). Pol Pot served both as the general secretary of the CPK and as the prime minister, holding the former until 1981 and the latter until 1979. Nuon Chea served as the CPK's deputy secretary. There were seven other high-ranking officials, and this elite group formed what is called the "Centre," the "Organization," or "Angkar." The CPK was fond of using numbers rather than titles as designations. For example, the Angkar operated out of Office 870 in Phnom Penh.

Nuon Chea, Deputy Secretary of the CPK

The use of numbers extended to the rest of the country as well, with regions divided by number. There were no more provinces; rather, the country was divided into seven geographic zones and two special regions. The seven zones were the Northwest, the North, the Northeast, the East, the Southwest, the West, and the Center. The special regions were the Kratie Special Region No. 505 and the Siem Reap Special Region No. 106. Each of the regions was subdivided into subregions, or *damban*.

Villages were divided into groups called *krom*, which contained between fifteen to twenty households. A *krom* was led by a leader called the *Meh Krom*.

The elites, that is, those people who became prominent in the new government, were a curious admixture of those who had studied in France and/or were students of Marxist/Leninist philosophy. That included Pol Pot, of course, but there was also Ieng Sary, the minister of foreign affairs; Khieu Thirith (or Ieng Thirith, Sary's wife and Pol Pot's sister-in-law), the minister of social affairs; Son Sen, who became the minister of defense, and Khieu Samphan, who was the chairman of the State Presidium.

### The Khmer Rouge Ideology

The Khmer Rouge believed in the principles of Marxist-Leninism and the teachings of Mao Zedong. This education taught that progress and change happen through successive revolutions. Some had the benefit of higher education in France, where they were taught Marxism. The Khmer Rouge also believed in their racial superiority. They banned any foreign influences, abolished the banking system, collectivized agriculture, and closed hospitals and schools. Education was virtually nonexistent. While the Khmer Rouge wanted the people to be literate and have basic knowledge, they didn't want their education to be tainted with Cambodia's past. They wanted to be in control of the information being disseminated.

The Khmer Rouge aimed to convert Cambodia into a country of obedient peasants. Agricultural products were raised in communes, and the state and its needs were more important than the family unit. If one had sex outside marriage, they could be executed, and one could only get married with the government's permission, as they didn't want people marrying outside their rank.

## The Role of Women

The Khmer Rouge boasted that work "liberated women," so they worked alongside the men and even children at times. The Khmer Rouge's position on this was derived from the work of the Marxist writer Friedrich Engels in his book, *The Origin of the Family, Private Property and the State*. Engels felt that women should perform industrial work and that the belief in the importance of the nuclear family should be abandoned in favor of the state. Engels saw the implementation of this as liberating for women. He believed her liberation would take place through participation in revolutionary activities. Furthermore, Mao Zedong stated that if such a change were to take place, the abolition of the inequalities between men and women "will follow as a natural consequence of victory in the political and economic struggles."

Some historians indicate the belief was that women would be trained to be productive members of their military forces. In the beginning, women were kept to behind-the-scenes roles, such as medical work and transportation. Over time, their roles became larger, even fighting on the frontlines themselves. Sum Sreng spoke of being taken from her family at the age of fourteen and sent to the frontlines. She described having escaped and running home to her parents, whom she dearly missed. However, she was always caught and returned to her unit. "I reached home five times. One time, I was sick—shaking, cold, hot temperature. They put me in a hammock and carried me back."

Democratic Kampuchea also promulgated a policy of breaking family bonds and traditional practices. Instead, the government wanted Cambodian peasants, in particular, to focus on the needs of the nation. The forced marriages pushed women to have sexual relations with, at times, strange men, and if they refused, their husbands and sometimes even Khmer Rouge officers would rape them. Predictably, the statistics of how many women were sexually assaulted were not kept track by the government. According to the Women and Transitional Justice in Cambodia project, which took an anonymous survey of those who lived through the Khmer Rouge regime, it is believed that almost 97 percent of women were forced into marriage. Around 80 percent of them were raped after they got married.

## Military

Democratic Kampuchea maintained a large standing army called the Revolutionary Army of Kampuchea (RAK). It had 230 battalions, which were split into 35 to 40 regiments and then subdivided into 12 to 14 brigades. The units of the military were led by three-person committees, with the ranking order going political commissar, military general, and the general's deputy. The political commissar wasn't really an army commander. Instead, they were there to make sure the unit followed the party's lines and ensure the government maintained control over the army.

The RAK operated throughout the various zones of the country, with each group assigned its own zone. As a result, a warlike atmosphere prevailed. If a member or members of any of these groups were judged to be "ideologically impure," purges took place to eliminate those undesirables, with troops crossing zones to make sure discipline was served. Their first assignment was to execute the FANK officers along with their families.

## International Relations

As one might expect, Democratic Kampuchea had close relations with China and, to a point, North Korea. They maintained contact with other countries as well, although very few were allowed to have embassies in the country. The only countries allowed to operate within the Khmer Rouge's borders were the aforementioned China and North Korea, as well as Egypt, Cuba, Albania, Laos, Romania, Vietnam (until the end of 1977), and Yugoslavia.

In 1977, Pol Pot made an official visit to China, where he was welcomed by Hua Guofeng, the premier of the People's Republic of China. He called Pol Pot the "Comrade from Cambodia." Pol Pot was treated to a visit to the agricultural area of China to present him with a model of agrarian accomplishment. Pol Pot also received approval for military aid from China.

## Religion

Democratic Kampuchea forbade the practice of religion, as it was, like other communist countries, an atheist state. As such, persecutions of people who practiced religions, such as Islam, Christianity, and Buddhism, took place. In fact, it has been reported that almost 25,000 Buddhist monks were executed during the Khmer Rouge regime. Despite the religious ban, some people practiced their religion in secret.

## The Atrocities and Genocide

It is believed the Khmer Rouge regime was one of the most brutal in recorded history, especially considering it was only in charge for around four years. A whole book could be written on the terrors the regime perpetrated against its people, so what follows only scratches the surface.

Between 1975 and 1979, the Cambodian genocide took place. They killed revered monks, attacked refugee camps, and destroyed Buddhist shrines, along with the surrounding neighborhoods. The Khmer Rouge executed the Chams and Vietnamese, as they sought to create a master race. If one spoke a foreign language, that almost always meant a death sentence. Sometimes, people were killed for wearing glasses, as that was a sign of intelligence. People could be killed for being absent at work, for scavenging for food, or for weeping over the dead. Executioners who hadn't reached their quotas were sometimes even executed. Journalists were assassinated, and babies were murdered. Despite the fact that the Khmer Rouge had control of Phnom Penh, they continually bombed it until it consisted of silent bloodied stones that couldn't speak of the horrors they'd witnessed.

Pol Pot believed that these harsh conditions, which included forced labor, starvation, and resettlement, would keep the people in line. People were overworked, and the sick were treated as if they were just a burden of society, with many of them dying. Those who were seen as non-contributors were often told, "Keeping you is no profit; losing you is no loss."

Although Article 9 of the Kampuchean constitution addressed justice and a court system, there was none. It was replaced by interrogations, security forces, and re-education centers. One such site was Tuol Sleng, which once was a high school and is now a genocide museum. There, people were tortured and forced to give up family and friends. Between 1976 and 1979, it is believed around 20,000 people were imprisoned there. In their rooms, they were shackled to prevent escape and forbidden to talk to each other, creating a true sense of isolation with no one to trust or confide in. Waterboarding was a common form of torture, as was being suffocated with plastic bags. Although the guards were encouraged to torture the prisoners, they were not supposed to kill them outright, but, of course, this still happened.

Those who died in the re-education camps, as well as others executed by the Khmer Rouge, were buried in the Killing Fields, which were located throughout all of Cambodia. Their victims would be buried in mass graves with no ceremony. Oftentimes, executions would be done with poison, sharpened sticks, or other blunt instruments, as this saved on ammunition. Sometimes, their victims would be forced to dig their own graves.

Pol Pot also regularly conducted purges. Khmer Republic officials who had served prior to the arrival of the Khmer Rouge were "tried" and executed, as were the officers of the FANK, who had served under the Khmer Republic.

There are no hard numbers when it comes to how many died under the Khmer Rouge regime. Numbers go as low as 1 million and go as high as nearly 3.5 million. Even the Khmer Rouge acknowledged 2 million people died, although they mainly contribute these deaths to the later Vietnamese invasion. It is startingly to look at these numbers, as scholars believe Cambodia had boasted a population of around 8 million people in 1975.

Historians disagree on whether what took place should be considered genocide. Some believe the actions of the Khmer Rouge didn't specifically target ethnic groups. According to Michael Vickery, these deaths were "largely the result of the spontaneous excesses of a vengeful, undisciplined peasant army." However, recent documents have come to light, showing that the Khmer Rouge willingly engaged in systematic mass killings. Even historian David Chandler states that ethnic minorities were not targeted specifically, but that doesn't seem to be the case. For instance, it has been estimated that half of the Cham Muslim population were killed during the Cambodian genocide. They were not allowed to practice their religion and were forced to eat pork, which goes against one of the tenets of Islam. If they refused to eat it, they were killed. They couldn't practice their language, and their children were taken to be raised as Khmers. The Chams were even renamed to Islamic Khmers, further stripping them of their heritage and ethnicity.

Victims of the Ba Chuc Massacre

## The Ba Chuc Massacre

From April 18ᵗʰ to April 30ᵗʰ, 1978, 3,157 civilians were brutally slaughtered in Ba Chuc, Vietnam. An additional 200 were either blown up or injured by land mines. It is believed only two people survived the massacre.

One of the survivors, a woman named Ha Thi Nga, said, "They shot my children one by one. My youngest, a two-year-old girl, was beaten three times but did not die, so they slammed her against a wall until she was dead." Her husband was shot and killed, and the soldiers tried to do the same to her. When the bullet didn't kill her, the soldiers bashed her in the head, leaving her to die. Miraculously, she survived.

This attack helped prompt the Vietnamese invasion of Cambodia, which took place later that year.

### The KUFNS

The acronym of KUFNS, also known by the French acronym of FUNSK, stood for the Kampuchea (or Khmer) United Front for National Salvation. It was a dissident group of Cambodians who were at odds with the leadership of Pol Pot. Their influence quickly spread, both in Cambodia and in Vietnam, after its formation at the beginning of December of 1978. It seems many people were not opposed to overturning Pol Pot's brutal government of repression.

The Salvation Front was also communist, but it opposed many of the principles extolled by the Communist Party of Kampuchea. Their goal was to rebuild the Cambodian areas that had been devastated by the many battles.

The KUFNS was led by Heng Samrin, who was the chairman, and Pen Sovan, who was the vice president. They played a vital role in the outcome of the fermenting hostilities.

### Cambodian-Vietnamese War, December 1978–September 1989

The third phase of Democratic Kampuchea manifested Pol Pot's deeply held suspicions of the Vietnamese. In fact, among the people who were purged were Vietnamese minorities who lived in Cambodia. He distrusted the Communist Party of Vietnam, which only increased when Vietnam signed a treaty of cooperation with Laos in 1977.

In 1977, tensions escalated between Vietnam and Kampuchea. By the end of the war, the Vietnamese were victorious over the Kampuchean troops. By early January 1978, the Vietnamese forces were only twenty-four miles away from Phnom Penh, but Vietnam withdrew its men. Despite this, Kampuchea declared it had won a major victory, even going on to claim that one Kampuchean soldier was equal to thirty Vietnamese soldiers. However, the Vietnamese, although they were poor, were well fed, while the Cambodians were half-starved. Vietnam also had more men standing by to fight (615,000 compared to Kampuchea's 70,000), as well as more tanks and aircraft.

Regardless, Kampuchea pushed on, holding Vietnamese territories and overrunning outposts in Ha Tien Province.

The clashes continued throughout the year while peace talks were attempted. However, there was no placating either side. By the end of the year, China was helping bolster Kampuchea's troops. The war itself officially broke out on December 21$^{st}$, 1978, when Vietnam sent in two divisions across the Cambodian-Vietnamese border, moving toward the town of Kratie in eastern Cambodia. The Kampuchean Revolutionary Army (KRA) wasn't able to repel the attack. Seeing the KRA's weakness, the People's Army of Vietnam (PAVN) launched a full-scale invasion, which consisted of around 150,000 soldiers, as well as heavy artillery and air support. The KRA fought back, even engaging in hand-to-hand combat when the need arose. Half of the KRA was wiped out after two weeks of vicious fighting.

Due to the heaving fighting, most of the Kampuchean leaders moved west. And it was a good move on their part, as on January 7$^{th}$, 1979, the PAVN entered Phnom Penh, along with members of the KUFNS. They set up a pro-Vietnamese state, which they called the People's Republic of Kampuchea.

The Khmer Rouge leaders took refuge in Thailand, and the Thai government housed them at the Khao Larn camp in Trat Province. In the meantime, the new Kampuchean government established its headquarters in Phnom Penh, where they started to rebuild the social and economic life of Cambodia. Unfortunately, the personnel who composed this new government lacked the skills and education to rebuild the country, as many of those familiar with politics and the like had been killed by the purges or fled elsewhere. In addition, there were anti-Vietnamese resistance groups that rioted against these officials.

United Nations Fiasco

The exiled Kampuchean government called for an emergency meeting of the United Nations Security Council, as Norodom Sihanouk wanted to make an appeal for the deposed government. He condemned Vietnam for violating the sovereignty of Cambodia, but he deliberately overlooked the human rights abuses that had taken place due to the Khmer Rouge. Furthermore, Sihanouk insisted that the UN not recognize this Vietnamese-installed government of Cambodia and to suspend any aid to them. While seven UN countries did approve of that resolution, the Soviet Union and Czechoslovakia opposed it, so the resolution was not passed.

In February of 1979, the new Kampuchean government and Vietnam held a meeting, after which the two signed a Treaty of Peace, Friendship and Cooperation. This treaty stated that there was a relationship between Vietnam and Cambodia. After the agreement was signed, the Soviet Union, the socialist countries of Eastern Europe, and India recognized the People's Republic of Kampuchea.

International arguments ensued, as both Democratic Kampuchea and the People's Republic of Kampuchea claimed the same seat at the UN. The UN committee in charge of such objections decided to recognize Democratic Kampuchea (Khmer Rouge) as the legitimate government of Cambodia. One of the reasons for this was China's strong support of the Khmer Rouge. In January of 1980, eighty members of the UN continued to recognize Democratic Kampuchea as the legitimate government, while the rest of the UN members recognized the new government, the People's Republic of Kampuchea.

Thailand, which had been harboring the Khmer leadership temporarily and had always feared Vietnam's expansion on the Indochinese Peninsula, demanded that Vietnam withdraw all its troops from Cambodia so the Cambodians themselves could elect a government of their own choosing. What's more, the Association of Southeast Asian Nations (ASEAN) believed the new Cambodian government would threaten the region's stability. China and North Korea agreed with this consensus.

In 1979, Deng Xiaoping was the leader of China. He rose to power after the death of Mao Zedong, whom he opposed, mainly on differences related to China's economic policies. In fact, Deng managed to manipulate the unseating of Hua Guofeng as the chairman of the Communist Party of China. Deng even told the American president at the time, Jimmy Carter, that he intended not to renew the Sino-Soviet Treaty of Friendship, Alliance and Mutual Assistance, which had been signed in the 1950s. He also announced that he was going to engage in a limited attack of Vietnam, as China supported the ousted Khmer Rouge regime. Deng also warned Moscow that, if necessary, he would launch a war against the Soviet Union. To demonstrate his seriousness, Deng stationed troops along the Sino-Soviet border.

### Sino-Vietnamese War, February–March 1979

In mid-February of 1979, China attacked Vietnam. China only had 200,000 troops enter Vietnam, while Vietnam had around 70,000. The Soviets assisted the Vietnamese in the war, but they only provided non-combat support.

The Chinese attacked from the west and east. In the west, troops planned to attack Cao Bang, Lang Son, and Quang Ninh Provinces. The forces in the east aimed to attack Hoang Lien Son, Ha Tuyen, and Lai Chau Provinces.

The People's Liberation Army (PLA) of China captured the heights above Lang Son. The Vietnamese, however, avoided direct combat, instead relying on guerilla tactics. On March 6th, Lang Son was taken. That same day, Deng declared that the "gate to Hanoi" was open and that the goals of the military campaign had been achieved. As China withdrew, it destroyed infrastructure and killed livestock in Vietnam, weakening Vietnam's economy in the process.

In the end, both sides claimed victory. China said it had crushed the Vietnamese resistance, while Vietnam stated it had driven off the invading troops. Both sides have varying estimates when it comes to casualties. It is believed that China suffered 26,000 deaths, while Vietnam had between 20,000 and 30,000 deaths.

Border skirmishes between the two countries continued for about ten more years, ending when Vietnam fully withdrew from Cambodia.

# Chapter 8 – Humanitarian Crisis

## The Refugee Camps and the "Land Bridge"

Throughout the 1980s, and even after the Cambodian-Vietnamese War ended, hundreds of thousands of Cambodians crossed into Vietnam in search of missing relatives and friends. Those who could sought refuge overseas. About 260,000 people relocated. While this was occurring, authorities didn't make any moves against the practice of Buddhism, allowing Buddhist schools to reopen. The people tried to reestablish the trade markets and businesses. Because few farmers were able to tend to their rice crops, a widespread famine broke out. The Vietnamese forces would consume what little rice there was. When some of the Cambodians managed to migrate to Thailand, the Thai people were astonished to see how emaciated and skeletal the Cambodian people were. It is believed at least 2.5 million Cambodians were at risk of starvation in 1980.

Border and refugee camps became commonplace. Sadly, politics and rivalries caused them to mimic the conflict going on around them, as the Vietnamese and the Khmer Rouge attacked some of them. A few camps became recruiting centers for the various hostile fighting forces in Cambodia. These camps were plagued by violence, rape, infighting, and depression due to the inactivity and the emotional distress the Cambodians were trying to cope with.

However, they also provided food and a small relief of safety. The government in Phnom Penh insisted that all aid be funneled through them, but distribution problems resulted, so aid agencies created the "land bridge," which bypassed the Cambodian government. By moving products on the "land bridge," camps could receive rice and other foodstuffs more efficiently. Approximately 150,000 metric tons of rice and other food arrived at the border camps as a result of this relief measure. The hungry Cambodians brought in their oxcarts, wagons, and bicycles for the food. Some aid groups objected to this "land bridge," as they felt it might encourage trade in the black market. It is also impossible to know how much food was actually distributed, as no solid records were kept by the camps that received the aid.

## The Nong Samet Refugee Camp

Cambodian warlords initially ran this camp, which was located just inside the Thai border. The warlords were accustomed to guerrilla warfare and ruled with an iron fist. For the most part, they controlled the food distribution.

In-Sakhan became the leader of the camp, who encouraged a thriving market, which attracted not only traders but also smugglers and black marketeers. The camp's population was a staggering 200,000. UNICEF and other aid agencies had been delivering much-needed relief to the camp, but they stopped once they heard In-Sakhan was hoarding it. Many people from Nong Samet went to a neighboring camp, as they had better luck receiving food there.

In time, it became necessary for the Thai army to remove In-Sakhan, doing so in July 1980. He was eventually replaced by Thou Thon. Thou Thon was a capable leader, and under him, the Nong Samet Camp became a recruiting center for the Khmer People's National Liberation Front, which opposed the Vietnamese-allied

People's Republic of Kampuchea in Cambodia. Thou Thon organized the members of Nong Samet, and they built roads and ditches and cleaned up sites. He created an efficient method for rice distribution, and he also chipped in with some of the work as well.

Eventually, in 1983, Nong Samet was incorporated into Site Two.

Market Stalls in Nong Samet Refugee Camp

*Cmacauley at English Wikipedia, CC BY-SA 3.0 <https://creativecommons.org/licenses/by-sa/3.0>, via Wikimedia Commons https://commons.wikimedia.org/wiki/File:Market_stalls.jpg*

## Site Two Refugee Camp

This camp was on the Cambodian-Thai border, and it was the largest of the refugee camps, as it accepted refugees from other camps that had been destroyed by hostile forces. It was overseen by the Royal Thai Government, the UN, and other UN-related organizations. The refugees were primarily from the Nong Samet, Bang Poo, Nong Chan, Nam Yeun, Sanro, O'Bok, Ban Sangae, and Dang Rek camps. Site Two was not used as a recruiting base; rather, it was a civilian camp for families and supporters of the Khmer People's National Liberation Armed Forces.

The Site Two programs provided medical care, public health, construction, sanitation, and skills training. The Thai did not want these camps to be permanent settlements, so they provided training to allow the people to move on and forge their own lives. These services were provided by international organizations, which included Christian Outreach, the Catholic Office for Emergency Relief and Refugees, the American Refugee Committee, and Doctors Without Borders.

As part of Thailand's rehabilitation program, they created schools and trained teachers. By early 1989, it is believed the camp had fifty schools with around 70,000 students.

Water was perhaps one of the biggest problems at Site Two, so UNBRO (United Nations Border Relief Operation) shipped water in until they could construct a reservoir. Dried beans, eggs, rice, vegetables, fish salt, oil, and wheat flour rations were given out to the residents on a weekly and monthly basis.

There were five hospitals at Site Two, but they acted more like clinics. These hospitals were not equipped with surgical tools, so if one needed surgery, they had to go to a local military hospital.

The Khmer Police temporarily provided security, but it had to be disbanded because it often violated human rights. Eventually, the Displaced Persons Protection Unit, a paramilitary group that was created solely to provide security on the border, took over. It was their function to not only maintain order but also to protect the camp from bandits.

Khao-I-Dang Holding Center

This refugee camp was on the eastern border of Thailand and administered by Thailand's Interior Ministry and the United Nations High Commissioner for Refugees. This camp came into existence after the Khmer Rouge regime fell. This facility actually had a surgical hospital, to which severely wounded or diseased patients came from other camps.

The camp had decent drainage, roads, latrines, and water tanks. It was supposed to be a temporary holding place for those who would be repatriated to other countries, including Cambodia. Approximately 4,800 arrived on November 21$^{st}$, 1979, the first day it opened, and that number rose to 84,800 by the end of the year. It hit its all-time high of 160,000 in March 1980, although it could have held as many as 300,000 people.

### Resettlement Issue in the Refugee Camps

Even though some of these camps sound fairly decent, especially when compared to Nong Samet's early days, one must remember that every camp was subject to violence, with both the Vietnamese and Cambodian forces shelling them. In time, Thailand declared the camps to be closed, but desperate Cambodians bribed their way in. After the hostilities ceased, the Cambodians remained in the camps, as they feared returning to their country. Instead, they preferred resettlement elsewhere. Between 1975 and 1997, around 153,000 Cambodians would make their home in the United States, with another 53,000 moving to France.

### The Restoration: People's Republic of Kampuchea

The People's Republic of Kampuchea (PRK) was a communist state that was at odds with the Khmer Rouge's Democratic Kampuchea. It wanted to put the brutality of the Khmer regime in the past and move forward.

Under the People's Republic of Kampuchea, ethnic minorities were to be respected. Those minorities included the Vietnamese living in Cambodia, the Cambodians from Thailand, the "Montagnards" of the northeast (also known as Khmer Loeu, an umbrella term for various ethnic groups), and the Cham people. There was also a Chinese minority living inside Cambodia, to whom the new republic did not extend protections, as China supported Democratic Kampuchea. As a result, the Chinese endured prejudice, and their native languages, Mandarin and Teochew, were only to be spoken among themselves.

The People's Republic of Kampuchea recognized Buddhism as the state religion. Temples were gradually rebuilt, and Buddhist festivals were celebrated. An order of monks was founded in Phnom Penh, and as time went by, other monasteries were established throughout the nation.

Since the UN refused to recognize the PRK, this government was disqualified from receiving international aid for supplies, food, and its reconstruction efforts. Of course, China refused to assist, as did the Association of Southeast Asian Nations (ASEAN). However, the Eastern Bloc countries sent a small amount of assistance. The Western nations sent most of their assistance to the refugee camps in Thailand. The United States provided $5 million per year in 1982, which was later increased to $8 million in 1984, then $12 million in 1987 and 1988, before dipping back down to $5 million again.

Due to the purges carried out by the Khmer Rouge, few Cambodian intellectuals were left in either Cambodia or in Thailand. They had very little desire to return home to Cambodia and sought new homes elsewhere, mainly in the Western countries. The PRK wanted its administrators, technicians, and bureaucrats to be adequately trained, but their efforts were hampered by the people's low level of basic education and skills. To make up for that deficiency, a number of the more promising candidates were sent to Eastern Bloc countries to study.

The Propaganda Wars

The People's Republic of Kampuchea conducted an ongoing propaganda campaign to rally national support. Billboards were papered with patriotic slogans and also depicted gruesome photos of the skulls of victims from the Khmer Rouge regime. The government further boasted that it had liberated the people from the repressive regime under Pol Pot. The annual Day of Remembrance, also called the "Day of Hatred," was instituted, with one of its slogans being, "We must absolutely prevent the return of the former blackness."

For the PRK, it was important to remind the people why it existed, especially since Pol Pot's Khmer Rouge resurfaced. During 1979, members of the Khmer Rouge began making their way back into Cambodia. They were supported by Thailand and China. This resurrection of the Khmer Rouge launched military actions along the Thai-Cambodian border, waging battles against the People's Republic of Kampuchea at various outposts.

It should be noted that Prince Sihanouk was still active during all of this. He had founded his own group, the National United Front for an Independent, Neutral, Peaceful and Cooperative Cambodia (FUNCINPEC), in 1981. By 1982, it had organized a resistance pact with the remaining members of the Khmer Rouge.

Dry Season Offensive of 1984-1985

During this offensive, the Vietnamese attacked the base camps of the anti-PRK forces who were in Cambodia, driving them into Thailand. The Vietnamese wanted to ensure they didn't enter Cambodia again, implementing the K5 Plan, which attempted to seal the entrances into the country by using trenches and minefields. However, the presence of the Vietnamese tended to ignite hostilities among the native Cambodians, so this Vietnamese assistance ended up backfiring on the PRK.

Although the PRK government had a team of military advisors from the Soviet Union, Cuba, and Vietnam, the PRK had a difficult time establishing a firm hold over the country. In 1986, Vietnam announced that it would begin to withdraw its occupation forces from Cambodia. It was a gradual withdrawal, taking place over a period of several years. In April of 1989, Hanoi and Phnom Penh jointly announced Vietnamese withdrawal from Cambodian soil.

### The Nascent State of Cambodia

Starting in that same year, 1989, the Soviet Union had started to collapse and therefore couldn't offer concrete military aid to Cambodia. Thus, the PRK had to consider making serious reforms to its economy and constitution.

In 1989, the National Assembly, led by Hun Sen, who became prime minister in 1984, decided to change the name of the country to the State of Cambodia. The armed forces were renamed the Cambodian People's Armed Forces. The country also began a series of economic and constitutional reforms. Free private ownership was permitted, along with a free-market approach. It was intended as a one-party state, but it allowed the palace to remain in Phnom Penh.

Sihanouk was not invited to become a king, especially seeing as he aligned himself with Democratic Kampuchea's National Government of Cambodia, which, as one might predict, had a communist flavor. This government also directly opposed the People's Republic of Kampuchea. After a series of talks, the new Cambodian government agreed to accept Norodom Sihanouk as the head of state—not as the king—in mid-1991.

### UNTAC

In October of 1991, the Paris Peace Agreements were signed, bringing an official end to the Cambodian-Vietnamese War. This coincided with the culmination of the Cold War between the United States and the Soviet Union, which would end only two months later. The meeting was fostered by the UN, which established the United Nations Transitional Authority (UNTAC) in Cambodia in 1992. Its purpose was to supervise a ceasefire, repatriate the displaced Khmers living along the Thai-Cambodian border, disarm factional politically-aligned armies, and prepare the country for free elections by 1993.

UNTAC had difficulty in getting the Khmer Rouge to cooperate, as they did not want to lay down their weapons. In 1993, general elections were held in Cambodia. About 90 percent of eligible voters participated. Norodom Sihanouk's son, Ranariddh, and his FUNCINPEC received the most votes. Hun Sen's Cambodian People's Party came in second, followed by candidates from the Buddhist Liberal Democratic Party. Prince Ranariddh and Hun Sen became the first prime minister and the second prime minister, respectively. The Khmer Rouge was formally outlawed in 1994 due to its violations of the Paris Peace Agreements.

A new constitution was drafted, and the government took the form of a constitutional monarchy, with Norodom Sihanouk as the king.

### 1997 Coup

Tensions between Norodom Ranariddh's FUNCINPEC and Hun Sen's Cambodian People's Party escalated over the years. On July 5th, military police aligned with the Cambodian People's Party surrounded a FUNCINPEC garrison and tried to get them to surrender, but they refused to do so. They also surrounded the residence of a FUNCINPEC general, but that also failed.

Hun Sen, who was away in Vietnam, returned after hearing this news and repelled the FUNCINPEC's counterattacks. The fighting lasted until September of 1997. Hun Sen then seized power, and Prince Ranariddh went into exile in Paris. Many members of the FUNCINPEC either fled the country or were shot.

In his report on human rights, Thomas Hammarberg, the United Nations Special Representative on Human Rights in Cambodia, reported that what had happened was a coup d'état. Hammarberg cited that the power-sharing formula, which had allowed for two major powers to exist at the same time, was one of the factors in the dispute. Hun Sen alleged that Ranariddh and his followers had been making alliances with former Khmer Rouge forces to fully take over the country. It should be noted that Hun Sen used former Khmer Rouge soldiers in his coup.

In 1998, the leaders of the FUNCINPEC returned for the general elections. The FUNCINPEC received 32 percent of the vote, while the Cambodian People's Party received 41 percent. The newly formed Sam Rainsy Party received 13 percent of the vote. The Cambodian People's Party didn't receive enough votes to form its own government, so it offered to form a coalition government with the FUNCINPEC and Sam Rainsy Party. However, both refused. Protests broke out, but eventually, a deal was brokered between the Cambodian People's Party and the FUNCINPEC. Hun Sen would be the prime minister (there would be no second prime minister), and Norodom Ranariddh would be the president of the National Assembly.

# Chapter 9 – 21st-Century Cambodia

In 2004, King Norodom Sihanouk, exhausted by the political crises, especially from that of Hun Sen of the Cambodian People's Party, became ill and resigned. His eldest son, Norodom Sihamoni, succeeded him.

Sihamoni spent his youth and young adulthood in Czechoslovakia. He was educated there, attending schools for the performing arts in Prague before studying filmmaking in North Korea. He later moved to France, where he taught ballet, eventually becoming the president of the Khmer Dance Association. While in France, Sihamoni was Cambodia's delegate to UNESCO.

Sihamoni remains the king in early 2021, and his prime minister is Hun Sen, who was a former Khmer Rouge leader until he defected in 1977. He is the longest-serving prime minister in the world, having taken office in 1985. In 2017, the National Assembly voted to abolish the minority leader and majority leader positions. Kem Sokha of the Cambodian National Rescue Party (CNRP) was the minority leader, having been appointed as such following a stint in prison for refusing to appear for questioning. Later that year, Hun accused Kem Sokha of collaborating with the United States to overthrow the government.

A month later, the Cambodian National Rescue Party, the main opposition to the Cambodian People Party, was banned due to these charges of treason. Charles Santiago, the chairman of ASEAN Parliamentarians for Human Rights, said this move was "the final nail in the coffin for Cambodian democracy."

## Communes

The communes are administrative divisions of Cambodia. They receive support from the World Bank, which funds the communes through its Sangkat Fund, which is a part of its Rural Investment and Local Governance Project. Its objective is to help reduce the poverty level of Cambodia.

The Sla commune in Takeo Province, located at the southern tip of Cambodia, has invested the funds in building canals to irrigate the lands. Besides rice paddies, some of the lands are devoted to growing cucumbers, sugar cane, and tomatoes, which they tend to grow during the dry season. Because of the canals, the farmers were able to increase their production by 20 percent.

The building of roads has also helped to increase the profitability of these communes. The Arak Trout commune of Kampong Cham Province in south-central Cambodia can transport its crops to market more efficiently than ever before. Not only that, but there is more accessibility to schools, temples, and health centers. Fifty-five percent of the villagers have even been able to afford to build houses.

Some of the people who belong to the communes have invested the funds in youth work. The Tboung Kropeu commune in Kampong Thom Province is raising awareness related to the dangers of drug use and provides youths with education on how to avoid street and rural gangs. Gangs are quite common in Cambodia, as they can be found even in small villages and towns. Drug addiction, prostitution, and gambling are also common, but communities throughout the country have been trying to take steps to temper their influence.

# OIL!

In 2000, Cambodia engaged in offshore oil exploration. Massive investments poured in, mainly from US-held Chevron Texaco, which spent over $20 million on the project. In 2006, Chevron confirmed that there were 700 million barrels of oil available and around 10 million cubic feet of natural gas.

In 2004, huge deposits of oil were discovered within the territorial Cambodia waters in the Gulf of Thailand. However, production stalled out when the government and the company failed to reach a revenue-sharing agreement. Chevron decided to sell its stake to Singapore's KrisEnergy in 2014. KrisEnergy holds a 95 percent stake in the profits from the oil production, while the government holds the rest. The oil drilling began in late 2020, and it is expected to produce 7,500 barrels a day once the initial drilling is completed and the rest of the wells come online.

According to the *Khmer Times*, Prime Minister Hun Sen announced that the Ministry of Education will use some of the profits from the oil production in Cambodia for education, primarily digital instruction, as well as developing and improving school infrastructure, including laboratories and computer rooms. However, others believe the money that comes from the oil production will only add to the corruption going on in Cambodia's government.

## Khmer Rouge Tribunal: Genocide and Violations of International Law

In conjunction with the United Nations, the Royal Government of Cambodia established a national court, using both local and foreign judges, to hear cases related to the Cambodian genocide and other international violations. All of the prominent people mentioned were indicted on the same day, September 15th, 2010, with varying counts of crimes against humanity, crimes of genocide, and the like.

## The Defendants

Kang Kek Iew was in charge of running prison camps, including the aforementioned Tuol Sleng, where they brutally interrogated prisoners. He was sentenced to life imprisonment for violations of human rights in 2010. Kang died after serving ten years.

Nuon Chea, the late Pol Pot's right-hand man (Pol Pot died in 1998), was charged with crimes against humanity, genocide, and war crimes. He was found guilty of numerous human rights violations and was sentenced to life imprisonment in 2014. In 2018, he was found guilty of genocide against the Cham people and the Vietnamese. Nuon died in 2019 while in the midst of appealing the 2018 case.

Khieu Samphan, who succeeded Pol Pot as the head of Democratic Kampuchea in 1987, was found guilty of crimes against humanity in 2014. Like Nuon Chea, he was also found guilty of the crime of genocide against the Vietnamese and Chams. Eighty-nine-year-old Khieu is currently serving a sentence of life imprisonment.

Khieu Samphan on the Stand

Although Ieng Sary was charged in 2010, he died before the case could be brought to a verdict. He passed away in 2013 at the age of eighty-seven.

Ieng Thirith, Ieng Sary's wife, was charged with a whopping forty crimes against humanity and twenty-seven war crimes, as well as six counts of genocide. The aforementioned men, excluding Kang Kek Iew, were charged with twelve crimes against humanity, six war crimes, and two counts of genocide. Ieng Thirith reportedly aided and abetted in the planning of and in the instigation of war crimes. In 2011, Ieng was found unfit to stand trial due to Alzheimer's, and she was released from prison in 2012. She died in 2015.

These were not the only ones to be indicted in the Khmer Tribunal. There was a total of nine people, although the remaining four were indicted in 2018 onward.

### Land Seizures and Protests

The Cambodian government has reportedly engaged in corruption, including the illegal sale of land to foreign investors, which resulted in the forcible eviction of many villagers from their properties.

A Cambodian land rights activist, Yorm Bopha, rose up in protest, especially in regard to the land development around Boeung Kak Lake near Phnom Penh. She claimed that Shukaku, a company owned by a senator from the Cambodian People's Party, filled much of the lake with sand after obtaining a ninety-nine-year lease to the property. According to Amnesty International, 20,000 residents were displaced by this action. As a result of Yorm's protests, the World Bank suspended aid to Cambodia in 2011 until the situation could be resolved.

In 2012, Yorm Bopha was picked up on allegedly fabricated charges of assault on two taxi drivers. She was arrested without warrants, and she was convicted of "intentional violence with aggravating circumstances" even though the people who said she "might be" the person later confirmed that she wasn't. Amnesty

International indicated that Yorm and her colleague, Tim Sakmony, who was also convicted, were "persecuted purely for their work defending the rights of those in their communities who have lost their houses through forced evictions." She was cleared in 2013 of these charges, but she was arrested again for the same offenses in 2016. She was sentenced to three years in prison and ordered to pay 2,500 US dollars (10 million riels).

**Urbanization and Economy**

The United Nations calls Cambodia a least developed country, meaning it meets the three criteria of poverty, human resource weakness, and economic vulnerability. Global sources have said that there is a lack of strategy on the part of the government to sustain healthy economic growth, which has resulted in the growth of poverty, congestion, crime, and violence. It has been reported that Phnom Penh has many of the same kinds of problems that affect overcrowded cities, including drug addiction and even human trafficking.

Most of the urban population lives and works around Phnom Penh, with some in secondary cities like Battambang, Siem Reap, and Sihanoukville. The cities suffer from rapid urbanization, especially in Phnom Penh and Sihanoukville, and financiers have warned that this sudden rise in urban development may lead to a real estate bubble. Overpricing is common due to speculation, which has raised concerns that limited resources will be eliminated. It has been said this also occurred in the neighboring country of Vietnam and even some areas of China.

In Sihanoukville, there is a number of casinos, which gave rise to hotels, restaurants, and tourist shops. A policy of "build first, license later" has brought about this uneven urbanization, which cannot be sustained by the available resources.

Special Economic Zones

Special Economic Zones are areas specially designated by the government where trade and business regulations differ from the normal rules. In those territories, there are incentives provided for businesses, including foreign ones, which enjoy reduced taxes and customs, as well as value-added benefits. The total investment in the special economic zones has been estimated to be about US$1.65 billion. Most of the projects were, and still are, financed and run by China.

## Critical Events of 2018

Prior to the July 2018 elections, in addition to the arrest of Kem Sokha, the Cambodian government curtailed media freedom, both offline and online. In 2017, authorities closed thirty-two FM radio frequencies that carried independent news programming, targeting those that featured *Radio Free Asia* and the *Voice of America*, which are both funded by the US. A day after Kem was arrested, *Cambodia Daily* was forced to close after it featured the headline "Descent into Outright Dictatorship," which focused on Kem's arrest. Although attempts have been made to block *Cambodia Daily*'s online presence, it continues to gain subscribers. In May 2018, *The Phnom Penh Post* was bought by a Malaysian businessman with ties to Hun Sen.

The 2018 Elections

As mentioned above, the National Assembly dissolved the major opposition party, the Cambodian National Rescue Party, in 2017, essentially leaving the country with a one-party system. Large numbers of those belonging to opposition parties fled the country to avoid arrest. Although this allowed them to maintain their safety, it also permitted Hun Sen and the Cambodian People's Party to secure all 125 seats in the National Assembly. Many countries, such as the US, Canada, the European Union, Japan, and Australia, have condemned the election, while China, Laos, and Thailand were among those who supported the results.

After the scrutiny by the international community, Hun Sen eased the pressure on his political opponents. The king pardoned fourteen members of the Cambodian National Rescue Party, who had been jailed for "insurrection." Tith Rorn, who was the son of a CNRP activist, died while incarcerated. Authorities claimed he died in a fall, but an examination of his body showed a broken neck and bruising.

### Human Rights Violations

In February 2018, a lèse-majesté law was passed, which makes insulting the monarch a punishable offense. This also applies to posts on Facebook.

The government has frequently resorted to repressive laws "to arbitrarily restrict the activities of human rights organizations and silence them," according to the Human Rights Watch. This includes amendments to the Cambodian constitution, one of which requires the government to take action against political parties if they do not "place the country and the nation's interest first." That statement, of course, is subject to interpretation.

In July of the following year, the Human Rights Watch claimed that two activists, Kong Raya (and his family) and Soung Neak Poan, were charged with incitement to commit a felony. Kong had participated in a commemoration ceremony for the murder of a political commentator, Kem Ley, by printing T-shirts in his memory and selling them online. Kem Ley was a prominent critic of the government, who was shot in broad daylight in 2016. Police detained Kong and some of his family members, forcing them to sign a confession. Soung Neak Poan was one of the supporters who gathered at where Kem Ley had been shot, distributing posters that called for the end of such killings. Unlike Kong, Soung refused to sign a confession.

Further, the Human Rights Watch Organization called upon the UN High Commissioner for Human Rights to "outline actions to be taken with regard to its international human rights obligations under the Paris Peace Accords signed back in 1991."

A number of countries in the European Union have threatened to eliminate special trade preferences. A European Commission was deployed to Cambodia to assess the country's compliance with its human rights obligations.

It should be noted this section only scratches the surface of what is happening in Cambodia today.

UN and International Reactions

The United States of America responded to that spate of attacks on human rights by suspending US$8.3 million in assistance programs. It also imposed visa restrictions against Cambodian officials involved with such policies. Furthermore, the US Treasury Department placed sanctions against the head of Hun Sen's bodyguard unit, the Hing Bun Hieng, for leading an "entity involved in serious human rights abuses."

Sweden, Cambodia's longest participating Western donor, stopped some of its development aid, except for research and education. The European Union, as well as its member states of Australia and South Korea, in addition to other democratic countries around the world, cut election assistance.

China, a country that has no competitive elections, praised Cambodia's elections and even sent in election observers. Japan, which did not approve of the results but is in competition with China for influence over Cambodia, provided US$7.5 million in electoral support but no election observers. In terms of aid, Japan indicated it would pledge $168 million for 2018.

China, on the other hand, sent Cambodia about $5.3 billion in investment and loan agreements. China also promised another $7 billion for new projects. In 2020, it was estimated Cambodia had an external debt of over $16.6 billion.

### Deforestation

While Cambodia has been credited with being one of the world's most forested countries that have not been drastically deforested, rapid deforestation is on the rise. It is such a problem in Cambodia that there are forest rangers who patrol the wooded areas. There are many impacts that came from deforestation, including the erosion of the topsoil, increased flooding, and climate change. In 2020, *The Phnom Penh Post* reported that there were almost 9,000 cases of what they call "natural resource" crimes. According to the article, people have been removing trees from protected areas in order to clear land for illegal private ownership. National authorities have placed some of the blame upon local authorities, saying that they colluded with the perpetrators.

However, they indicated some of these crimes are occurring "because traders have come to buy timber, and as people lack jobs and owe money to banks, they have resorted to illegal logging."

### Water Resource Management

In December of every year, Cambodians produce Prahok fish paste, which is a staple in their diet. The freshwater Tonle Sap is a great source of fish. However, partly due to deforestation, the level of the lake has been starkly declining. According to the magazine *ASEAN Today,* "the freshwater fish catch among some of the country's licensed fishers has dropped 31% compared to last year." Cambodia's yearly fish catch is worth approximately US$600 million annually.

Under normal conditions, the Tonle Sap drains into the Mekong River in the dry season. When monsoon season comes, the Mekong River flows backward, filling the lake back up. In 2020, the water that flowed back into the lake was down a quarter from its average levels. It is believed nearly one-third of Tonle Sap's natural habitats have disappeared between 1993 and 2018. The Fisheries Action Coalition Team reported that the level had dropped too fast for the fish to reach full maturity. One of the fishermen, Sim Suom from Siem Reap, said, "Children in this community go to work in factories now because there are no fish in the lake."

There are numerous factors that play a role in this, including climate change and the erection of two new dams in Laos.

Floating Fishing Boat on Tonle Sap

In early 2021, Cambodia and its neighboring country to the north, Thailand, have been inflicted with a severe ecological threat from China's decision to hold back the Mekong River at the Jinghong Hydropower Station for about a month. China claimed it reduced the water flow because of "maintenance for the transmission lines of the power grid," according to the *South China Morning Post.* John Roberts of the Golden Triangle Asian Elephant Foundation indicated that Thailand and the countries downstream from there, including Cambodia, depend upon predictable flooding to service their harvests and fishing industry. Since the year 2008, he added that "natural floods were crucial for renewal of ecosystems and provided critical habitat for fish, waterfowl and wildlife." The activist group and the Mekong River Commission reported that droughts are occurring in the lower reaches of the river. They did, however, concede that some of that was due to climate change.

Brian Eyler, the co-head of the Mekong Dam Monitor, a project partly funded by the US State Department, warned that China's withholding of this upstream water came without sufficient warning or transparency. "No one had time to prepare for the river dropping nearly one meter overnight. China needs to provide notification in a much more timely manner and as take downstream needs into deeper consideration and demonstrate a higher level of accountability in the region," Eyler said.

According to the World Bank, there have been some recent successes in sustaining a potable water supply in Phnom Penh. They have four water treatment plants there and an envious distribution system. Critics, though, have pointed out the fact that this hasn't been done in moderately-sized cities.

In some cities, like Sihanoukville, urban development is uneven. Some constructions of high-rise developments have been too rapid, which has placed a strain on the water supply. In addition, complaints erupted when the water was cut off at various phases in the erection of these projects.

### Flood Protection, Drainage, and Waste Management

The opposite problem has also occurred, as Cambodia is subject to a cycle of monsoons and dry spells. Areas around Phnom Penh and Battambang, which are on the banks of Tonle Sap, are vulnerable to floods during the rainy season. On occasion, there have been more severe monsoons and typhoons. Sihanoukville is affected adversely by a rise in the sea level, and its lack of adequate drainage is exacerbated by inadequate solid waste management. Only 44 percent of the population in the urban areas are connected to a sewer system. The remaining people use septic tanks, but it is up to the individual property owners to maintain those tanks. In Phnom Penh, there is a limited landfill capacity, and the projections of the people's needs have proven to be incorrect, as it reached capacity in 2020. The Royal Government of Cambodia has admitted it faces difficulties in the area of waste management and has called for a Wastewater Management Law to resolve this problem.

Some of the solid waste management services have been subcontracted to private companies, but they indicated that solid waste is wrongfully deposited along roadways and public spaces, particularly in Siem Reap. The government doesn't compensate those companies for their losses in their clean-up efforts, and, unfortunately, some of it remains undone.

### Exports

In 2020, Cambodia exported US$4 billion in agricultural products. These exports include milled and paddy rice, mangos, cashew nuts, rubber, bananas, and Pailin longan. Pailin longan are very sweet, small, beige-colored fruits. In return, Cambodia imports vehicles, machinery, and animal feed from the US.

The *Khmer Times* reports that Cambodia exported $526 million of goods to the United States in 2020, which was a 32 percent increase from the prior year. The goods are being exported according to the Generalized System of Preferences, a bilateral trade agreement between the two countries.

# Conclusion

Cambodia remains a country in crisis. Over the centuries, its soil has been trampled upon by foreigners who have made Cambodia a battleground. Through the years, Cambodia has reached out to other countries, like France, Vietnam, China, and the United States, to form mutually-satisfying alliances, only to be betrayed or abandoned in time. It is a country besieged with broken promises, but it is still often criticized because the Cambodians have found political or ideological solutions in less popular and old-time philosophies. Often, Cambodia has been promised protection in exchange for their labor and goods only to incur exploitation. Even their own leaders have done that. Much of its precious past has been shrouded due to neglect by others or its own heads of state.

The Cambodians have truly been through a lot, even in recent years. The genocidal regime of the Khmer Rouge has left a tragic and indelible mark upon the people. Because it was a battlefield for many decades, climate change and the country's perennial battle with the monsoons and dry seasons pose serious humanitarian threats they are unprepared to handle. The water management system set up by their old kings is in serious disrepair, but, with foreign help, it is in the process of rehabilitation. This has allowed for increased tourism to their country and religious sites, for Cambodia truly is a beautiful country worth exploring.

However, the Cambodians themselves are bent upon survival. Cambodia has been described by analysts as a "vaguely communist free-market state with a relatively authoritarian coalition ruling over a superficial democracy." In addition, it is alleged that Cambodia is one of the most corrupt nations in Asia. It has a low-income economy, with two million people living in poverty, and it is likely this number will increase due to the COVID pandemic. Only time will tell if the Cambodians will be able to reinvigorate their economy and embrace more democratic ideals.

# Here's another book by Captivating History that you might like

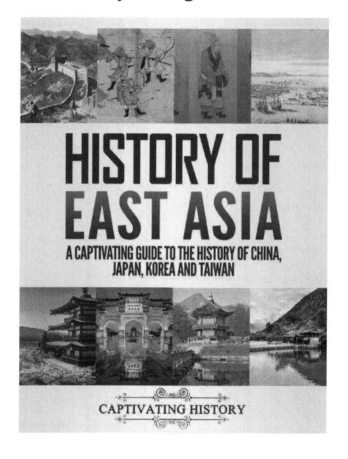

# Free Bonus from Captivating History (Available for a Limited time)

Hi History Lovers!

Now you have a chance to join our exclusive history list so you can get your first history ebook for free as well as discounts and a potential to get more history books for free! Simply visit the link below to join.

Captivatinghistory.com/ebook

Also, make sure to follow us on Facebook, Twitter and Youtube by searching for Captivating History.

# Bibliography

"Angkor Dynasty". Retrieved from
http://www7.plala.or.jp/seareview/newpage2Chapter4Angkor.html.

"Assassination of Resident General Bardez".

"ASEAN at the Crossroads". Retrieved from
https://www.phnompenhpost.com/opinion/asean-crossroads-nam-has-
no-alternative.

Cady, J. (1966). *Thailand, Burma, Laos and Cambodia.* New Jersey
Press

Cady, J. (1964). *Southeast Asia: Its Historical Development.*

"Cambodia: Achieving the Potential of Urbanization, August 2018".
Retrieved from
http://documents1.worldbank.org/curated/en/580101540583913800/p
df/127247-REVISED-CambodiaUrbanizationReportEnfinal.pdf.

"Cambodia". Retrieved from
http://countrystudies.us/cambodia/6.htm.

"Cambodian Election: Ruling Party Claims Landslide in Vote with No
Main Opposition". Retrieved from https://www.bbc.com/news/world-
asia-44999358.

Chandler, D. (2009). *A History of Cambodia (4ᵗʰ ed.)*. Westview Press.

Coedes, G. (1966). *The Making of Southeast Asia*. New York.

Harrison, B. (1960). *Southeast Asia: A Short History*. London

Karakia, Z. (1973). *Failure through Neglect*.

"Khmer Empire: The Ancient History Encyclopedia". Retrieved from https://www.ancient.eu/Khmer_Empire/.

Kiernan, B. (2008). *Blood and Soil: Modern-Day Genocide 1500-2000*.

"The Legend of Preah Ko and Preah Keo". Retrieved from http://arcmthailand.com/documents/documentcenter/THE%20LEGEND%20OF%20PREAH%20KO%20PREAH%20KEO%20AND%20ITS%20INFLUENCE%20ON.pdf.

"Ministry Revises Safe Village Policy". Retrieved from https://opendevelopmentcambodia.net/news/ministry-revises-safe-village-commune-policy/#!/story=post-146295.

Stark, M.; Griffin, P.; Phourn, C; Ledgewood, J, et. al. (1999) "Results of the 1995-1996

Archeological Field Investigations at Angkor Borei Asian Perspectives. #38".

"The World Bank Empowering Cambodian Communes". Retrieved from https://www.worldbank.org/en/news/feature/2011/04/12/empowering-cambodian-communes.

Tarling, N. (1999). *The Cambridge History of Southeast Asia*.

Vickery, M. (2000). *Cambodia 1975-1982*. Silkworm Books.

Made in the USA
Columbia, SC
15 November 2022

71294665R00070